The Gospel of Inclusion

The Gospel of Inclusion

A Christian Case for LGBT+ Inclusion in the Church

Brandan J. Robertson

Foreword by David P. Gushee

CASCADE *Books* · Eugene, Oregon

THE GOSPEL OF INCLUSION
A Christian Case for LGBT+ Inclusion in the Church

Cascade Books
An Imprint of Wipf and Stock Publishers
199 W. 8th Ave., Suite 3
Eugene, OR 97401

www.wipfandstock.com

PAPERBACK ISBN: 978-1-5326-7609-3
HARDCOVER ISBN: 978-1-5326-7610-9
EBOOK ISBN: 978-1-5326-7611-6

Cataloguing-in-Publication data:

Names: Robertson, Brandan, author. | Gushee, David, 1962–, foreword writer

Title: The gospel of inclusion : a case for LGBT+ inclusion in the church / Brandan J. Robertson, with a foreword by David Gushee.

Description: Eugene, OR: Cascade Books, 2019 | Includes bibliographical references.

Identifiers: ISBN 978-1-5326-7609-3 (paperback) | ISBN 978-1-5326-7610-9 (hardcover) | ISBN 978-1-5326-7611-6 (ebook)

Subjects: LCSH: Sexual orientation—Religious aspects—Christianity | Gender identity—Religious aspects—Christianity | Homosexuality—Religious aspects—Christianity | Church and the world

Classification: BV625 R63 2019 (paperback) | BV625 (ebook)

Manufactured in the U.S.A.   04/02/19

To every LGBT+ person who is struggling to reconcile their faith and sexuality—may this book help you to begin to see and know, deep in your bones, that you are loved and worthy of love *just as you are.*

Contents

Foreword

The Christian Bible has been interpreted for centuries by dominant Christian groups in ways that harm people, both within and outside the Christian church. The harmed groups have included Jews, Muslims, indigenous people, African slaves, colonized people, black people, women, those deemed heretical or unorthodox in their beliefs, and gender and sexual minorities—the latter including groups now generally called lesbian, gay, bisexual, transgender, intersex, and queer.

Much of the most important theology and ethics that has been published and widely disseminated in the last seventy-five years (since World War II) has emerged from previously harmed groups. All, in one way or another, have simply demanded that dominant Christians stop hurting them. Movements that began in protest have then almost always matured into offering alternative renderings of the Christian faith, alternative readings of Christian Scripture, and alternative understandings of Christian ethics. They have moved from protest theologies to constructive theologies—at least, that is one way to describe the trajectory.

Today, we know these alternative constructive theologies as, for example, liberation theology, black theology, indigenous theology, feminist theology, womanist theology, Latinx theology, Asian-American theology, and so on.

Brandan Robertson's offering here strikes me as a transitional work between LGBTQ protest theology and what is now maturing under the label "queer theology." The first generation of LGBTQ protest theology emerged in mainline and Roman Catholic Christianity in the late 1960s and 1970s. But this kind of literature (with a few exceptions) emerged much later in evangelical Christianity, in the late 2000s and 2010s. Much of this work was defensive; that is, it defended LGBTQ people from harm done by traditionalist Christianity and sought to defang the traditional repertoire of biblical verses most often cited to stigmatize and reject them.

Brandan does some of that defend-and-defang work here, but it is not really his focus. That's good, because that approach allows traditionalist interpreters to set the agenda, and this has rarely worked out well for those who are harmed by traditionalist Christianity.

Rather quickly, Brandan moves off the adversaries' playing field and onto his own more interesting ground. For example, he argues that traditionalist and so-called inerrantist biblical interpretation hardly resembles the approach to the sacred text that either Jesus or Paul took, and looks much more like their adversaries' way of reading Scripture. He centers attention on deep, pervasive patriarchy in the ancient world—and therefore in the ancient biblical texts—as fundamental both to understanding what is going on with these texts and as a reason to reject any literalist application of them. He offers a most creative interpretation of the emasculation of the multiply pierced Jesus on the cross. And he offers a focus on the marks of the inclusive kingdom of God and the movement of God's Spirit, both in the New Testament and among LGBTQ Christians today.

In these ways Brandan's work contributes to next-generation constructive queer theology; that is, theology coming out of LGBTQ experience that is moving past protest to mature alternative renderings of Christian theology and ethics. This theology is now taking its place within the panoply of other such theologies. It is no coincidence, for example, that most theologies emerging from the margins of white-straight-male-colonial-Christianity challenge (selective) biblical literalism and test the fruits of dominant Christianities by their impact on marginalized individuals and groups. Each of these theologies emphasizes the significance of the social location of Christianity's interpreters, attends to power dynamics in the Christian community, and emphasizes that the biblical text is always interpreted by human beings, who are never infallible. And in the end, all these theologies move toward an understanding of the Christian gospel that emphasizes God's loving and just intent to liberate the oppressed and create a better world through Jesus Christ. And that looks a lot like the Jesus we meet in the Gospel accounts, even if it does not look as much like the theologies of, say, Luther and Calvin.

What we are seeing in this next-gen theology written by queer people is yet one more historically marginalized and deeply harmed group of people claiming Jesus for themselves—even, if necessary, against the diktats of traditionalist Christianity.

One does not have to agree with every interpretive theological or ethical move in this book to be glad to see its overall message—that, once again, the sublime love, justice, and mercy of Jesus is proving more far-reaching than some of his most ardent defenders are prepared to accept. Which means that millions of people who have been taught to fear Jesus as their enemy are going to be able to welcome him as their greatest friend, indeed, as their Savior and Lord, their Rock and their Redeemer.

That is Good News indeed.

David P. Gushee
Distinguished Professor of Christian Ethics at Mercer University
and Immediate Past President of the American Academy of
Religion

Acknowledgements

This book comes as a product of over eight years of in-depth research and study of the biblical texts and Greco-Roman culture. Over those eight years, so many brilliant scholars and theologians have taken time to help me develop my understanding of all of the information available on these topics. I wish to thank Dr. Jenny Barry, Dr. Leonard Martini, Dr. J. R. Daniel Kirk, Dr. Miguel De La Torre, Dr. David Gushee, Dr. Kathrine Turpin, Rev. Annanda Barclay, Dr. Floyd Thompkins and Matthew Vines for the conversations, debates, and direction they provided as I worked my way to the conclusions presented in these pages. Your pioneering and brave work on these topics has helped multitudes find their place once again at the table of grace—*thank you.*

To the team at Wipf and Stock publishers for being committed to publishing a wide array of perspectives on topics like this, and especially to my editor Robin Parry, whose theological insights not only on this project but in his own writings have shaped my faith in profound ways—*thank you.*

To our gracious Creator who has crafted the vast array of humanity in your own image and likeness and who continues to call us into a deeper understanding of who we are and you are— may you be honored and glorified in these pages.

Introduction
Shifting Our Approach

There is no topic that has divided Western Christianity more in the past decade than the topic of the full inclusion of sexual and gender minorities (otherwise known as the LGBT+ community[1]) into the ecclesial life of Christian denominations around the world. As the LGBT+ rights movement gained tremendous momentum through the 1960s and, in many ways, culminated on June 26, 2015 with the national legalization of same-sex marriage by the Supreme Court of the United States, large portions of Christianity have struggled to keep up with the rapid cultural, social, and legal changes, unsure of how to reconcile their doctrinal beliefs with modern psychological data and the widespread social acceptance of the spectrum of queer[2] sexualities and gender identities.

This has resulted in two predominate responses from within Christian denominations. Either the denominations have dug their heels into the ground and declared that they are not open to reconsidering their beliefs on this topic, suggesting that the matter has been settled by the teaching of Scripture and the tradition of

---

1. "LGBT+" is common vernacular that stands for lesbian, gay, bisexual, transgender, and other queer sexualities or gender identities.

2. The word "queer" is a common label used by many within the LGBT+ community to describe the full umbrella of gender identities and sexual orientations that fall under the traditional LGBT+ label. Queer can also refer exclusively to gender non-conforming individuals who do not fit into the male/female binary.

the church, or they have largely adopted what has become disparagingly called the "revisionist"[3] approach to biblical teachings on homosexuality, seeking to reinterpret the meaning of biblical passages referring to same-sex sexual relations, suggesting that they either do not apply to Christians in the new covenant era or that we have misunderstood the original meaning of the Greek and Hebrew language and context.

While both of these approaches have legitimacy in the theological discourse around LGBT+ inclusion, they also largely have failed to convince anyone to change their perspective. The conservative (or "traditionalist") approach works for evangelicals and other conservative Christians who uphold the doctrine of the inerrancy of Scripture, and settles the conversation there.[4] The revisionist approach works for those who are seeking to continue working within the boundaries set by the traditionalist arguments, centered on the six biblical texts that refer to homosexuality,[5] and attempts to settle the conversation with the assertion that we have misunderstood what was happening in the mind and context of the biblical author, or that the biblical texts offer little perspective on the modern understanding of sexuality and gender identity.[6]

When we keep our debate on LGBT+ inclusion rooted in our interpretation of the six biblical verses relating to homosexuality, we are missing the forest for the trees. There is little movement possible for either side of the debate because we are so focused on whose interpretation of these verses is the most historically and theologically correct, which is a question that can never yield a

3. "Revisionist" tends to refer to attempts to revise our understandings of the original meaning of the Scriptures. See Gonnerman, "Why Matthew Vines Is Wrong about the Bible and Homosexuality."

4. For examples of the traditionalist approach, see the work of Robert Gagnon, Michael Brown, Preston Sprinkle, Albert Mohler, Kevin DeYoung, Sam Allberry, and Christopher Yuan.

5. The six biblical passages traditionally used to condemn "homosexuality" are: Genesis 19:5; Leviticus 18:22 & 20:13; Romans 1:26–27; 1 Corinthians 6:9; 1 Timothy 1:9–10.

6. For examples that contain the revisionist approach, see the work of Matthew Vines, Colby Martin, Walter Wink, Justin Lee, and Robin Scroggs.

firm and conclusive answer, for no one can access the mind of the biblical authors. Instead of focusing on these verses as the center-point of our discussion, I believe we must instead step back and observe the metanarrative of Scripture and Christian theology, and ask if the broader scope of Christian teaching has anything to say to us about the inclusion of sexual and gender minorities in the life of the church. This approach has been embraced by many theological movements throughout the history of Christianity, and has fostered the birth of liberation theology, feminist theol-ogy, eco-theology, and in recent years has been repurposed and reapplied to the queer context.

As an LGBT+ person who has grown up and been trained in conservative evangelical contexts, I have spent the past decade of my life wrestling with reconciling my faith with my sexual identity. I have undergone conversion therapy programs, consulted with leading theologians on the topic, and traveled around the world seeking answers to the theological question of whether or not there is a Christian case that can be made for the affirmation and full inclusion of sexual and gender minorities into Christianity and in society. As my journey has unfolded, I have become convinced that the ethical trajectory of the Bible should lead Christians towards a position of greater inclusion and acceptance of those who have previously been considered "unclean," and that the New Testament imperative of Jesus is to listen to and rely on the ongo-ing revelation of the Holy Spirit to guide our faith and practice. I have also grown increasingly aware of the great psychological and spiritual harm that non-inclusive theology produces in the lives of LGBT+ individuals who find themselves in conservative reli-gious contexts, and I believe that the "fruit" that is manifested by non-inclusion is a strong indictment against its validity as good theology and practice.

While my own faith and theological paradigm has undergone much evolution and reformation over the last decade, I still feel a special call to work within the theological paradigm of evangelical Christianity to make a biblical and theological case for the mod-ern work of the Holy Spirit in expanding the boundaries of the "kingdom of God" to fully include sexual and gender minorities. In this book, I will explore the effects of non-inclusive theology and practice and explore the redemptive trajectory of Scripture towards greater inclusion. After exploring the context of the six so-called "clobber passages" and highlighting a sample of biblical passages that demonstrate the need for Spirit-led reformation towards inclusion, I will conclude by sampling modern sociological evidence that suggests that the Holy Spirit is, in fact, igniting a revival among sexual and gender minorities in Christian communities around the world.

At the beginning, I want to state that this book does not seek to provide a comprehensive theology of sexuality and gender from a progressive Christian perspective, but rather to provide an accessible entry point for those seeking to understanding how the Bible and Christian tradition provide a path for the inclusion and embrace of LGBT+ people. This book is intended to serve as a companion to my previously published work, *Our Witness: The Unheard Stories of LGBT+ Christians*. That volume includes a sampling of the arguments contained in this book but it wasn't the appropriate project for me to flesh out those arguments in any depth. My goal in this book is revisit some of the arguments I touched on in *Our Witness*, and then to create a theologically robust yet accessible guide for LGBT+ Christians and our allies to articulate a progressive Christian theological case for LGBT+ inclusion and affirmation in the church. It is my prayer that all who pick up this text will be provoked and encouraged to dig deeper into the rich Christian tradition of inclusion and fortified in the fight against non-inclusive theologies that for too long have claimed to be the only legitimate Christian position on LGBT+ inclusion. Our tradition gives us strong ground to stand upon in our fight for a place for LGBT+ Christians at the table of grace, and we should stand with confidence and conviction as we declare the radically inclusive gospel of Jesus Christ in our day and age.

I

Known by Your Fruits
The Harm of Non-Inclusive Theology

Before we begin any discussion exploring a pro-inclusion Christian theology, I believe it's important to highlight the negative impact of non-inclusive theologies on the individuals subjected to such teachings. One of the most basic biblical tests for determining the truth of a doctrine or practice is based on the teaching of Jesus in the Gospel of Matthew where he proclaims that one way his disciples can determine between true prophets and false prophets is "by their fruits."[1] This language of "fruits" appears numerous times throughout the New Testament[2] and plays off of familiar first-century agricultural imagery, which suggests that some crops yield "good fruits," or a harvest that is luscious, edible, and profitable, compared to those crops that yield "bad fruits," or a harvest that is diseased and scarce. Throughout the New Testament we are continually reminded that faithful followers of Jesus will bear "good fruits," or what the apostle Paul calls

---

1. Matthew 7:16.

2. Matthew 3:8–10; 7:16–20; 12:33; 21:43; Luke 6:43; John 15:5; Romans 7:4; Galatians 5:22.

"fruits of the Spirit."[3] If one takes this call to discernment and examination of Christian teaching seriously, it naturally leads one to ask the question "what is the result of a teaching on the lives of those who receive it?" If a teaching produces life and love, one could make the case that it bears good fruits, and therefore is a faithful and true teaching. Jesus' own life serves as our example of what good fruit looks like: standing up for the oppressed, welcoming the marginalized, and healing those who have been harmed by religious and political powers. But what if a teaching produces death, mental harm, and fear? It seems, following the pattern set forth in the Scriptures, that we should condemn this teaching because of its "bad fruit" and it should be "cut down and thrown into the fire"[4] or hastily disregarded as "false."

The Psychological Evidence of Harm

Yet, when it comes to the teachings of the church about non-inclusion, this biblical standard has been largely disregarded. Over the past decade, dozens of peer-reviewed studies have been done that have demonstrated a clear link to non-inclusive religious teachings and practices to higher rates of depression and suicide in sexual and gender minorities. In 2008, Dr. Louis Hoffman released a paper describing a multi-year research effort to determine what, if any, psychological harm was caused by the religious teachings an LGBT+ person heard. He concluded his findings with the following statement: "it is evident that negative and ambiguous religious statements do impact the spiritual, religious, and particularly the psychological health of LGBT individuals."[5]

In 2012, the European Symposium of Suicide and Suicidal Behavior released a groundbreaking survey that suggested that suicide rates among LGBT+ youth were significantly higher if the

3. Galatians 5:22.

4. Matthew 7:19.

5. "Religious Belief and Perceptions of Psychological Health in LGBT Individuals."

youth grew up in a religious context.[6] Similarly, dozens of studies from 2001–2015 have found links between religious affiliation and higher rates of depression and suicidality among LGBT+ adults. A study published in 2014 by Jeremy Gibbs concluded:

> [Sexual Minority Youth] who mature in religious contexts, which facilitate identity conflict, are at higher odds for suicidal thoughts and suicide attempt compared to other SMY.[7]

A study published in the *American Journal of Preventative Medicine* found that religious affiliation significantly increased the risk of suicide among LGBT+ youth, while it generally decreased the risk for suicide among heterosexual youth. Carol Kuruvilla, a reporter for the *Huffington Post*, summarized the findings of the study, saying:

> . . . for lesbian and gay youth, increasing levels of religious importance were associated with increased odds of recent suicidal ideation. In fact, lesbian and gay youth who said that religion was important to them were 38 percent more likely to have had recent suicidal thoughts, compared to lesbian and gay youth who reported religion was less important. Religiosity among lesbians alone was linked to a 52 percent increased chance of recent suicidal ideation.[8]

Even the non-affirming gay Christian scholar Christopher Yuan released the results from a study he conducted of students who identify as LGBT+ at Christian colleges, which found that students who attended non-affirming Christians schools, "felt lonely as LGB or [same-sex attracted] Christians . . . as if they were social outcasts."[9]

---

6. Jewish Press Staff, "Study: Highest Suicide Rates among Religious Homosexuals."

7. Goldbach, *Growing Up Queer and Religious.*

8. Kuruvilla, "Chilling Study Sums Up Link between Religion and Suicide for Queer Youth."

9. Yuan, "Giving a Voice to the Voiceless," 58.

Every year, new studies come out that suggest that non-inclusive religious teachings result in higher rates of depression and suicidal ideation among LGBT+ youth and adults alike. These facts must be heeded by those in Christian leadership and cause deep reflection on how their teaching and practices are complicit in these concerning trends.

Counting the Costs

While many conservative religious commentators have strongly pushed back against any suggestion that their theology has any actual effect on LGBT+ mental health and suicide rates, and in fact, will often use these statistics to suggest that it is not their teachings but rather the "gay lifestyle" that contributes to the mental distress of LGBT+ people,[10] these numbers and the experiences of LGBT+ people simply cannot be denied or ignored. Religious teachings that perpetuate the idea that sexual and gender minorities are somehow disordered, flawed, or sinful because of this piece of their identity has direct effects on the mental health of such individuals. Likewise, when straight congregants digest these teachings and are left to implement them practically in their own lives as they relate to LGBT+ people, it often translates to harsh rejection and condemnation. If the LGBT+ person is a youth, they may be forced into reparative therapy programs, a pseudo-psychological practice that has been condemned by every reputable[11] psychological association in the United States as dangerous to the health and wellbeing of LGBT+ people.[12] If a youth chooses to embrace

---

10. For examples, see Dr. Michael Brown's interview where he suggest LGBT+ rights activists use suicide victims as pawns to perpetuate the gay agenda. Tashman, "Michael Brown."

11. By "reputable," I am referring to psychological associations that engage in peer-reviewed studies and have been validated by the government as reliable sources of information, as opposed to the many smaller, religiously rooted psychological associations that are seen by the mainstream psychological community as engaging in a form of pseudo-psychology.

12. Human Rights Campaign, "Policy and Position Statements on Conversion Therapy."

their sexuality or gender identity, they are likely to be kicked out of their homes, driving up the rates of LGBT+ youth homelessness, which currently represents between 20–40 percent of all homeless youth.[13]

As one examines the evidence closely, the fruit of non-inclusive religious teaching and practice is undeniably clear—it breeds death, rejection, and severe psychological and spiritual damage on sexual and gender minorities. It follows that because of this bad fruit, these teachings should be "cast into the fire"[14] and religious practitioners of all stripes should be led back to their sacred texts and traditions to reassess the messages they are preaching, seeking to listen closely to the voice of the Spirit for a message that is truly good news and brings life to all people.

13. Nicholas, "Lesbian, Gay, Bisexual, and Transgender Youth: An Epidemic of Homelessness."

14. Matthew 7:19.

2

Clobbered

Reexamining Biblical Texts
on Homosexuality

While it is clear from the abundant psychological evidence that the traditional Christian teaching which condemns homosexuality is inherently harmful to the psyche of LGBT+ individuals who sit beneath its weight, it is essential to begin to dismantle this non-inclusive teaching by examining how it mishandles and misunderstands the biblical texts that *seem* to address the topic of homosexuality. But as with so many modern topics, the Bible actually says very little about homosexuality. In fact, I want to suggest that the Bible says *absolutely nothing* about modern same-sex relationships as we know them.

I say this primarily because the notion of sexual orientation was not even understood until the sixteenth century, meaning that the writers of Scripture would not have known or thought in terms of the categories of "heterosexuality" and "homosexuality." The Bible does, however, make a few references to same-sex sexual experiences, and it is from these limited passages that the church has constructed an anti-affirming theology. The Bible does, however, make a few references to same-sex sexual experiences, and it is from these limited passages that the church has constructed an anti-affirming theology.

In the entirety of the Bible, from Genesis to Revelation, there are 23,145 verses of Scripture. Of those 23,145, there are only *five* that say *anything* of same-sex sexual relationships. These five verses are:

- Leviticus 18:22

- Leviticus 20:13

- Romans 1:26–27

- 1 Corinthians 6:9–10

- 1 Timothy 1:9–10

On my own journey to reconcile my Christian faith and my queer sexuality, I must admit that the hermeneutical arguments made about these five verses were not what convinced me that there was no contradiction between my faith and sexuality. As you will see, there are very good reasons to believe that these texts, when understood in their scriptural and cultural contexts, do not apply *at all* to the modern conversation about LGBT+ inclusion in the church. On the other hand, I have no problem conceding that for some of these texts, particularly the Leviticus passages, their interpretation in the ancient world would have been a flat condemnation of all forms of queer sexual expression. I agree with scholar William Loaders assessment that "the Bible roundly condemns homosexuality and homosexual activity. Of this there is not a shadow of doubt. Its writers deplored homosexual acts as a deliberate perversion of human nature, a flouting of God's intention in creation."[1]

As we will explore in significant depth later, the patriarchal worldview that the authors of Scripture function within demanded that they condemn all queer forms of sexuality and gender because such expressions fundamentally threatened the ordering of their society. So, if a modern gay couple were to appear within the

---

1. Loader, "What Does The Bible Say about Homosexuality?"

historical context of the ancient Hebrew people, it is quite possible that they would have been horrifically "put to death,"[2] as Leviticus commands, because of the threat their relationship posed to what the Hebrew people would have seen as the fundamental ordering of creation. In order to come to a place of full-affirmation and celebration of LGBT+ identities from a Judeo-Christian perspective, it seems to me that the only logical and faithful path is to discover more faithful ways of relating to Scripture as a whole (meaning, understanding its historical and cultural context and applying it in a non-literalistic, non-inerrantist way), and to chart the trajectory of inclusion that the Spirit seems to be drawing the narrative of Scripture towards from the earliest pages of Genesis to the final words of John in Revelation.

With that said, I *do* believe that understanding the context of each of the so-called "clobber passages" is essential to combat their misuse and abuse by non-affirming Christians. As my former Bible professor Dr. Christopher Yuan always said, "Context isn't just king, it's the whole deck of cards." When we understand the context of each passage and how the ancient culture understood homosexual sexual expression, we will begin to see that in almost every instance, the condemnation had less to do with romantic relationship between two people of the same sex, and more to do with more severe sins such as idolatry, exploitation, and threatening the "divine ordering" of ancient society.

As we examine the biblical "clobber" passages, I will examine the scriptural and cultural context, as well as the word choices that the author uses to show how a simplistic, face-value reading of isolated texts can lead us to interpretations that are not wholly faithful to the authorial intent, and can lead to severe misuse and abuse of these passages.

2. Leviticus 18:22.

THE HEBREW BIBLE

SODOM AND GOMMORAH

An important passage of Scripture that has often been used to make non-affirming arguments is the story of Sodom and Gomorrah in Genesis 18 and 19. In these chapters we are told of two angelic messengers who meet Lot at the town gateway and desire to spend the night in the town square. Lot, knowing that the cities were filled with wicked people and desiring to show hospitality insists that the messengers stay with him in his home. Late in the evening, men from the cities arrive at Lot's door, demanding that the messengers come outside so that they can rape them. Astonishingly, Lot refuses to send out the messengers and instead offers his daughters to then mob instead. The story concludes with the angelic messengers making the mob blind, allowing Lot and his family to escape before they called down God's judgment, through fire and brimstone, on the city.

For millennia, uninformed readers of this text have tied the destruction of Sodom and Gomorrah to the mob of men's desire to have sex with the messengers sent to Lot's house. It is from this story that the idea and word "sodomy" was birthed, which is defined simply as the act of sexual penetration between two men. Yet nearly every modern commentator and scholar on this text, both traditionalist and affirming, argue that the sins for which Sodom and Gomorrah were judged for was *not* homosexuality or "sodomy," but for the cities' lack of hospitality.

In the ancient Near East, the code of hospitality was at the core of their conceptions of morality. Even in Middle Eastern cultures today, radical hospitality is an integral part of their cultural expression. As we read about the state of affairs in ancient Sodom and Gomorrah in the book of Genesis, we learn that the people of these cities were proud, selfish, and self-indulgent. They cared about their own needs rather than the needs of those around them.

In Genesis 19 we even get a glimpse into how they treated foreigners (the angelic messengers)—they attempted to gang rape them in a show of dominance and uncontrolled sexual "passion." This stands in stark contrast to the code of hospitality for most Middle Eastern cultures, which instructs people to welcome travelers and foreigners with open arms. Lot represents this code well, offering to welcome the men, cook them a meal, and ensure their safety, while the men of his town display grand immorality. Later on in the Hebrew Bible, this inhospitable posture is declared to be the sin for which Sodom is destroyed: "Behold, this was the guilt of your sister Sodom: she and her daughter had pride, excess of food, and prosperous ease, but did not aid the poor and the needy. They were haughty and did an abomination before me. So, I removed them when I saw it."[3]

Again, we see that the writer of Ezekiel is highlighting that Sodom was destroyed because of their pride, which led them to be selfish and inhospitable, rather than aiding the poor and the needy in their midst. This point is later echoed in the New Testament book of Hebrews where the writer says: "Do not neglect to show hospitality for strangers, for by doing that some have entertained angels without knowing it."[4]

This text clearly references the Sodom and Gomorrah narrative and warns that we should be hospitable to everyone we encounter, for we never know when we might be entertaining angels in disguise. The clear teaching here is that Christians should always seek to extend hospitality to everyone they encounter, regardless of their place of origin, as both an ethical imperative and a means of be prepared for potentially interacting with messengers from God.

Traditionalists often will assert that the New Testament passage of Jude 7 stands in contrast to this interpretation of the Sodom and Gomorrah narrative. Jude 7 states: ". . . just as Sodom and Gomorrah and the surrounding cities, which likewise indulged

3. Ezekiel 16:49–50.
4. Hebrews 13:2.

in sexual immorality and pursued unnatural flesh, serve as an example by undergoing a punishment of eternal fire."[5]

Any reader of the Sodom and Gomorrah narrative can clearly see that the "unnatural flesh" that the mob was pursuing was the flesh of angels, which were otherworldly beings that were, in fact, unnatural from an earthly perspective. The unnatural sexual desire of the men of Sodom and Gomorrah was that they attempted to gang rape foreigners who actually turned out to be God's angelic messengers. The actions of the mob display egregious sexual immorality on many levels, but there is certainly no clear indication in any text relating to the Sodom and Gomorrah narrative that the mobs so-called "homosexual desires" were understood to be the reason for God's judgment of the city.

Leviticus 18:22 and 20:13

> 18:22 *You shall not lie with a male as with a woman; it is an abomination.*

> 20:13 *If a man lies with a male as with a woman, both of them have committed an abomination; they shall surely be put to death; their blood is upon them.*

The two key "clobber" passages in the Hebrew Bible come from the Book of Leviticus. As I have examined these texts, I have come to the conclusion that in general these two verses may indeed be a condemnation of any form of same-sex sexual relationships. This primarily had to do with the patriarchal lens that the Hebrew people adopted as their worldview. I will explain later why I think the trajectory of Scripture leads us away from patriarchy towards an egalitarian, just and equal world. But for our Hebrew forerunners in faith, their worldview was patriarchal and thus they viewed God, sex, and relationships through that lens.

However, in order to understand each passage, knowing the cultural context is still vitally important. Both of these verses in

5. Jude 7.

Leviticus are directly preceded by reminders that these rules were meant to keep the Hebrew people from being like the worshippers of Molech, the Canaanites and the Egyptians, the surrounding dominant polytheistic cultures.[6] Some scholarship suggests that both cultures worshiped gods of fertility and love, such as Astarte and Ishtar, and part of the worship of these gods included sexual sacrifice. It was believed that by depositing semen into the body of a priest or priestess of the goddess would lead one to a prosperous and eternal life.[7] In Egypt, worship to the god Molech and the goddess Ashtoreth involved rituals in which individuals of both sexes would have sex with one another to worship and appease these deities. Anti-LGBT+ scholar Robert Gagnon writes about an institutionalized and acceptable practice that occurred in ancient Mesopotamia where male cult prostitutes to the goddess Ishtar are described as dressing up like women and dancing in public processions, taking the passive position in same-sex sexual relationships.[8] Even if such sexual worship was not always common in these cultures (this is a hotly debated assertion), we do know that in the ancient Egyptian culture it was at least fairly common for the Egyptians to rape men whom they had conquered.[9]

There were clearly practices in many ancient cultures surrounding the Jewish people where same-sex sexual intercourse was common, and at times even celebrated, in relation to either worship of pagan deities or as an act of aggression and dominance over conquered people.

The Jewish purity codes emerge in an incredibly narrow context, one meant to be applied among the small collection of tribes that was the Hebrew people at the time of its writing. Most of the codes relating to sexual relationships and expression throughout the entire Torah are centered on preventing the Jewish people from

---

6. Leviticus 18:2–3; 20:2

7. For more on the practice of sacred prostitution, see Kramer, *The Sacred Marriage Rite*; Marcovich, "From Ishtar to Aphrodite"; Day, "Does the Old Testament Refer to Sacred Prostitution and Did It Actual Exist in Ancient Israel?"

8. Gagnon, *The Bible and Homosexual Practice*, 48–49.

9. Walsh, "Leviticus 18:22 and 20:13: Who is Doing What to Whom?" 208.

engaging in sexual acts between members of the same family. In fact, the context of Leviticus 18:22 is in the midst of prohibitions about incest and therefore would be more accurately interpreted in this light. To further this line of reasoning, it should also be noted that in the Book of Deuteronomy, where a summary of the key moral codes are given to the Jewish people, there is not *one* condemnation of same-sex sexual relationships at all, but numerous condemnations of incest.[10] Clearly, the context and application of the prohibition of same-sex sexual relationships was so narrow within the context of the ancient Hebrew people that it did not bear repeating elsewhere in the laws and codes of the Hebrew Bible.

The entire Jewish purity code emerged for a single purpose: to distinguish the Jewish people as the worshippers of the one true God from all other cultures, which was an incredibly difficult task for a small group of tribes of ex-nomadic and often-colonized people. The codes were established less as a solid standard of morality for all time and more as a direct response to the cultural threats that surrounded the Hebrew people in the ancient world.

This is also why time and time again the New Testament makes a strong distinction between "the law" and "the Spirit." Under the new covenant of Jesus Christ, the purity laws became of no use, for the plan of God was seen to be expanding from making a covenant with one chosen race of people to *all of humanity*. Therefore, holding all of humanity to cultural laws would have been an incredibly difficult task and a hindrance to the spread of the gospel around the world.

Both Jesus and Paul pushed heavily against the "legalists" who sought to both limit adherence to the messianic community to culturally Jewish individuals and require any gentile converts to begin adopting Jewish cultural standards. Paul calls these standards "stumbling blocks"[11] and demands that no Christian should place these standards in the path of a person seeking to follow Jesus. All were welcome to come and follow the path of Jesus, while keeping

10. For an extensive study on this, check out Kalir, "Same-Sex Marriage and Jewish Law?"

11. Romans 14:13.

and adapting their own culture and customs to the wisdom they found in the teachings of the new Christian movement.

Scholar William Loader concludes that interpreting the Levitical prohibitions against homosexual sexual relations as nonbinding is actually the most faithful posture Christians can take, saying:

> [P]eople arguing that [homosexual] sexuality should be respected as we respect that of heterosexuals with no further restrictions, do operate with a hermeneutic which operates similarly to that of Jesus, Paul, and Mark. Citing the biblical texts to counter such a hermeneutic similarly could, indeed, put one unwittingly in the wrong first-century company, including among those who already charged Paul with just seeking to placate the people of his day.[12]

All of the primary figures in the New Testament find themselves being accused of transgressing the laws of the Hebrew Bible, and as we will explore later, almost all of them are quite happy to declare that such laws were incomplete and inadequate, falling short of God's truest ethical desires for humanity. For the person embracing the New Testament ethic of Jesus and Paul, it becomes increasingly difficult to claim *any* of the Levitical purity codes as binding or even relevant to the life of the Christian today.

When we understand the cultural context from which the prohibitions taught by Jewish purity law emerge, and understand the context of the literature that these prohibitions are found within, it becomes abundantly clear that the writers of Leviticus were clearly thinking of homosexual sex acts *within the context of pagan cultural customs or worship*. The express intention of the purity laws was to distinguish the Hebrew people from pagans that surrounded them. They were primarily *cultural* standards, not eternal moral law, and the ethic of the New Testament calls Christians away from seeking to uphold these standards. Instead, Christians are to embrace the Spirit beneath the laws—the Spirit of Love.

---

12. Loader, "Biblical Perspectives on Homosexuality and Leadership," np.

THE NEW TESTAMENT

Romans 1:26–27

> *For this reason, God gave them up to dishonorable pas-sions. For their women exchanged natural relations for those that are contrary to nature; and the men likewise gave up natural relations with women and were consumed with passion for one another, men committing shameless acts with men and receiving in themselves the due penalty for their error.*

Paul's condemnation in The Epistle to the Romans seems pretty clear to the average reader—he is referring to some sort of sexual relationship between people of the same-sex, both men and wom-en, and declaring it to be sinful. But again, when reading any bibli-cal text, it is wrong to assume that the text is speaking about any modern-day equivalent of whatever may seem to be referenced.

Before we engage these verses, its vital understand the textual context of these condemnation. Paul's entire point in his opening of this letter is to call out the church at Rome for its judgmental attitude towards pagans: he is convicting them of their own sin of judgment. As Richard Hays writes:

> The passage builds a crescendo of condemnation, de-claring God's wrath upon human unrighteousness, using rhetoric characteristic of Jewish polemic against Gentile immorality. It whips the reader into a frenzy of indignation against others: those unbelievers, those idol-worshipers, those immoral enemies of God. But then the sting strikes in Romans 2:1: "Therefore you have no excuse, whoever you are, when you judge others; for in passing judgment on another you condemn yourself because you, the judge, are doing the very same things." The reader who gleefully joins in the condemnation of the unrighteousness is "without excuse" (2:1) before God just as those who refuse to acknowledge God are "with-out excuse" (1:20).[13]

13. Hays, "Awaiting the Redemption of our Bodies," 9.

This context is vitally important. Paul is calling on the Christian readers of his epistle to be wary of the sin of judgmentalism that we are all prone to fall into. Yes, he does call out the sinfulness of the gentiles and there must a conversation about what exactly the sins Paul was addressing refer to, but before anyone engages Romans 1 to explore what it may say about homosexuality, it is essential that we begin our efforts with a posture of non-judgment, the very point of this text.

The Descent of Pagan Culture

First and foremost, in Romans 1 Paul is describing the decent of the Roman culture away from the one true God and into pagan idolatry. He says that in the beginning, Roman people, like all people, knew the true and living God, but for some reason decided to turn to polytheistic idolatry, which leads them down an immoral descent into "unnatural" and "pagan" ways of being in the world. Paul, being a faithful Jew, is harkening back to the same teaching that we found in the Levitical passages: that the cultures surrounding the righteous people of God has fallen away from a innate knowledge of God and into destructive patterns of sin through idolatry, and God's people should resist the influence of these cultures at all costs.

Most scholars believe Paul is writing the letter to the church at Rome from Corinth, the second most prominent city in the Roman Empire. In both Corinth and Rome, as well as throughout the entire Greco-Roman world, worship of the great mother goddess, known as the Magna Mater, was one of the primary religious and cultural practices. Throughout any city in the Greco-Roman world, thousands of priests and priestesses of Aphrodite, Cybele, Artemis, and Venus could be seen, and at the center of every major city one could find a large temple dedicated to one of these prominent goddesses. Scholar Lynn Roller describes the importance of these cults, saying:

By the first century C.E. the Magna Mater was thus a divinity with a central place in Roman life. . . . The prominence of the Magna Mater in literature, art, and practice speaks of a cult that lay at the very center of the Roman religious experience. Her temple was located in the heart of the city, near its most venerable shrines.[14]

The worship of these goddesses usually involved sacred sex, where priests and priestesses would engage in sexual activities ranging from anal sex, penetration by phallus, and oral sex as an act of worship to the goddess. The male priests were almost always effeminate, cross-dressing, and were commonly castrated, preventing them from performing their "natural" sexual role, which rendered them less-than-men in the Greco-Roman patriarchal consciousness, a concept I'll explore later in this book. The temple priests and priestesses often lived together, as a marginalized community in their patriarchal society, and would engage in regular sexual activity. The second-century writer Apuleius describes the lifestyle of these priests in this sultry vignette:

> The eunuch, whose name was Philebus, led me off to his lodging. When he reached the door, he called out: "Look, girls, Look! I have brought you a lovely new man-servant!" The girls were a set of disgusting young eunuch priests who broke into falsetto screams and hysterical giggles of joy, thinking that Philebus really meant what he said, and that they would have a fine time with me.[15]

There is no doubt that to much of the general society and the fledgling Christian movement alike, the lifestyle embodied by these priests and priestesses was immoral, although it was generally accepted in the Greco-Roman world as what could be called a "necessary evil"; after all, they needed someone to appease the goddess. But in Paul's mind, as well as in the consciousness of much of the ancient world, sex was seen as an act for procreative purposes only. Sex was not intended for pleasure, it was not intended to bring connection or intimacy to couples; it was for the purpose of

14. Roller, *In Search of God the Mother*, 315–16.
15. Apulieus, *Golden Ass*, 188–89.

producing offspring, period. Therefore, any sexual activity that did not accomplish that end, or worse, wasted the ejaculate of a man, was seen as impure and unnatural. Natural sex was procreative, and everything else was unnatural. It makes perfect sense, then, that Paul condemns the pagan culture of the Greco-Roman world that begins with idolatry and moves towards sacred sexual rituals that do not produce offspring. Paul writes:

> For their women exchanged natural relations for those that are contrary to nature; and the men likewise gave up natural relations with women and were consumed with passion for one another, men committing shameless acts with men and receiving in themselves the due penalty for their error.

Notice what Paul *doesn't* say: he doesn't say that women had sex with other women, contrary to what is often assumed by readers. Woman-on-woman sex was rare in the ancient world, and even if it was practiced, it was usually ignored as benign. Paul does say that women engaged in idolatry—a reference to the priestesses of the various Magna Mater cults—and exchanged natural relations for those contrary to nature, meaning that women engaging in ritual sexual activities whose goals were not procreative. He then says that the men—a reference to the priests of the various Magna Mater cults—exchanged natural (procreative) relations with women and committed unnatural, "shameless" acts with other men. In the cultural context, it is clear that what Paul is referring to by "natural" and "unnatural" is an understanding of sex that limited to procreation, and for which Paul rightly condemns the temple priests and priestesses for freely and proudly engaging in such practices. In this paradigm, their idolatrous actions were indeed against nature.

One of the key interpretative problems for modern Christians who seek to use this passage as a condemnation of homosexuality is that almost no Christian church today upholds the sexual ethic that Paul is arguing for. Most Christians today believe that sex is primarily meant for procreation, but is also to be used for pleasure and for building relational intimacy. We no longer believe that semen is a "sacred" substance and that the "wasting" of it constitutes a grave moral sin. Most Protestant Christian theologians and ethicists would say that condoms, masturbation, oral sex, and anal sex are all permissible in the context of marriage—yet all of these acts would fall squarely in the category of "unnatural" to the apostle Paul. If the church desires to be consistent in using Romans 1 to condemn homosexuality as unnatural, it must also be willing to condemn *all* non-procreative sexual activities as equally sinful, a task I am positive that most Protestant Christian leaders are not willing to take up.

It is also important to note that in Romans 1:26–27, Paul's writing is limited to a *particular culture*—the unsanctified pagan Roman way of living—and *not* the general human condition. He is writing about a *specific* people in a *specific* context. After all, not all of humanity has followed the same trajectory Paul outlines in this first chapter—it was unique to hie Greco-Roman context and culture. Male same-sex sexual relations were quite common in the Greco-Roman world that Paul lived in,[16] but most of the expressions of same-sex sexual activity were linked to pagan temple worship, pagan dinner parties known as *convivias*,[17] prostitution, abuse of slaves, or pederasty.[18] Scholar Lynn Roller comments on just how common these priests and practices were in Paul's world:

> The evidence suggests that eunuch priests were a common sight in Rome. The prominence of these priests in Roman society may have resulted from the secure position given to eunuchs by the Magna Mater cult. Such a protected status could have caused their number to multiply, as the priested proved a magnet for transsexuals,

16. Dover, *Greek Homosexuality*.

17. "Convivia" were common Roman dinner parties that often turned to drunken orgies.

18. Pederasty refers to an ancient practice of an older man taking a prepubescent boy as a sort of apprentice. In this relationship the older man would engage in sexual relations with the boy. This practice did not threaten the patriarchal norms of the day because the boys used in these relationships were not yet considered "masculine" because they had no facial hair and were not fully grown.

transvestites, and others who found themselves on the margins of society.[19]

Therefore, to universalize Paul's condemnations in Romans 1 to apply to all of humanity for all time is not a faithful reading of the text. The cultural and scriptural context here is clearly pagan idolatry occurring in Rome, and he is condemning same-sex sexual relationships offered as a result of worship to false gods. The kind of sexual encounter Paul is condemning in Romans 1 is clearly *not* that found in modern homosexual relationships, about which he says nothing, but rather idolatrous sexual expression unique to the pagan Roman context. Consequently, it cannot be used to condemn the loving, committed relationships of LGBT+ people today.

Furthermore, when we examine the words that Paul uses in his condemnation of this exploitative same-sex behavior, there are more significant reasons to deduce that his condemnation has nothing to do with the kinds of relationships found among modern LGBT+ people. First, its essential to note that Paul's condemnation of same-sex sex is on the basis of its being *shameful*, not sinful. Paul was a faithful Jewish believer and was well trained in the Levitical laws. We know from his other writings that Paul struggled to understand how the Jewish tradition should relate to this new spiritual community he was building, centered around the example and teachings of Jesus. Paul eventually concludes that the purity laws of the Hebrew Bible are of no benefit to the gentile Christians, and forcefully opposes any suggestion that gentile followers of Christ need to become Jewish through rituals or adherence to purity codes. But Paul fluctuates significantly throughout his letters on this point.

In Romans 1, Paul seems to be echoing the purity codes of Leviticus—saying that same-sex intercourse was shameful because it made one impure according to the purity code. Same-sex sex was clearly not shameful in Greco-Roman culture: it was practiced fairly openly and was generally accepted in certain cultural and

19. Roller, *In Search of God the Mother*, 319.

ritual contexts. In Greco-Roman culture, men were allowed to have sex with other men, so long as they were lower on the social hierarchy. The immoral act would have been if a Roman man allowed himself to penetrate or be penetrated by another man of the same social status—this would be seen as an act of emasculation and would be condemned by everyone in their patriarchal society.

Another popular argument against an anti-LGBT interpretation of Romans 1 centers on another interpretation of the word "unnatural." Scholar John Boswell first postulated that perhaps what Paul means by nature is that straight men and women were having sex with other straight men and women, and thus, were acting contrary to their nature. Any transgression against the way we have been fashioned, then, could be seen as sinful and worthy of condemnation in this interpretation. While this argument makes linguistic and logical sense, there are stronger theological cases that can be made to suggest that Paul is not saying that homosexuality is against the natural ordering of the world. But what is clear is that when Paul uses the word unnatural, he is clearly referring to the sexual acts themselves, and not the fundamental nature of the person committing them. As stated above, in the Greco-Roman context it would have been seen as unnatural for two men of equal status to engage in sexual intercourse, or any person to engage in sexual activity that was not procreative. The act itself was unnatural, going against the natural ordering of Roman society and God's design for sex, not the nature or orientation of the human committing the act.

Biblical scholar Jeremy Punt shows how the same Greek word used in Romans 1 for "nature" is used by Paul later in Romans 9–11 in a positive light, describing God acting out of accordance with nature by grafting the gentiles into the chosen people. Punt writes:

> Paul's argument on the inclusion of Gentiles in the people of God in Romans 9–11 is reliant upon the same contrast between what is natural and what is unnatural. By using the same language and having God as the implicit author of the cutting and the grafting, it is God acting against

nature and Paul defending his gracious nature without claiming it to be natural. Moreover, by the same token, the followers of God are expected to follow suit: to act contrary to nature![20]

Clearly, then, Paul doesn't see the word "nature" as denoting something fundamentally sinful or immoral, but rather, something that it out of the ordinary. It's a morally neutral term. What Paul seems to be doing throughout the entire Epistle is making a case for why the gentiles need salvation in Christ and why they should be included into the church, and he does this by beginning his argument with a dramatic portrait of the way in which gentiles have turned from God and act in ways contrary to what was seen as "normal" or out of step with God's intended design. In Romans 1:26–27, Paul is seeking to call the gentiles away from sexual behaviors that exploit each other or cause them to reflect the broader, idolatrous, gentile culture. When viewed in light of the cultural context of first-century Rome and the whole message of the Epistle, it becomes clear that the version of same-sex sexual relationships Paul is speaking about are *not* reflective of modern LGBT+ relationships, of which Paul had no awareness whatsoever, and therefore he cannot be used to condemn such relationships.[21]

1 Corinthians 6:9–10

> *Do you not know that wrongdoers will not inherit the kingdom of God? Do not be deceived! Fornicators, idolaters, adulterers, **male prostitutes, sodomites**, thieves, the greedy, drunkards, revelers, and robbers—none of these will inherit the kingdom of God.*

The words Paul uses in 1 Corinthians 6:9, which are mistranslated above as "male prostitutes" and "sodomites," are the Greek terms *malakoi* and *arsenokoitai*. I will explore *malakoi* later in this section,

20. Punt, "Romans 1:18–32 amidst the Gay-Debate."

21 For an in-depth look at the sexual practices of the Greco-Roman cults, read Townsley, "Paul, the Goddess Religions, and Queer Sects: Romans 1:23-28."

but for our purposes in exploring the meaning of 1 Corinthians 6:9, we should look at the word *arsenokoitai*, which is literally a made-up word never once found in ancient literature until *after* Paul's usage of it. Most biblical scholars agree that Paul created this term after looking at the Greek translation of Leviticus 18:22 and 20:13, which in Greek are rendered in the following way:

> Leviticus 18:22—*meta arsenos ou koimethese koiten gynaikos*
>
> Leviticus 20:13—*hos an koimethe meta arsenos koiten gynaikos*

The literal translation of the term is *"man bed"* and most scholars agree that this again likely refers to some form of ritual rape or temple prostitution, as we've previously discussed in our interpretation of the Leviticus passages. However, anyone who tries to claim that they definitively know what Paul's usage of this term means is simply being dishonest—its lack of historical usage makes it impossible to definitively understand.

The word *arsenokoitai* is only used a few times in Greek literature after Paul introduces it in his epistles. One of those external sources is the *Sibylline Oracle* 2.70–77, where it occurs in a list of "economic sins," or sins rooted in the economic exploitation of others:

> Do not steal seeds. Whoever takes for himself is accursed for generations of generations, to the scattering of life. Do not *arsenokoitein*, do not betray information, and do not murder. Give one who has labored his wage. Do not oppress the poor man. Take heed of your speech. Keep a secret matter in your heart.

Again, most scholars agree that this again likely refers to some form of ritual rape[22] or temple prostitution. But it is highly unlikely, contextually, to assume that *arsenokoitein* is referring to a committed sexual relationship between two consenting partners

---

22. In the sacred sexual rituals of many ancient religions, a woman would be required to offer herself as a sexual sacrifice to a god or goddess, and would be offered money by a man in exchange for sexual intercourse.

of the same sex. This interpretation is also the most likely case because there are literally *dozens* of other well-known words in first-century Greek vernacular that the apostle Paul could have used to describe same-sex relationships and sex and chose intentionally not to. Here's a brief overview of some of the choices Paul had:

- *arrenomanes*—meaning mad after men or boy-crazy.

- *dihetaristriai*—a synonym referencing female-on-female sex.

- *erastes*—a sometimes older man who loves a sometimes younger male.

- *erōmenos*—a sometimes younger male who loves an older male.

- *euryproktoi*—men who dress as women, also a vulgar reference to anal penetration.

- *frictrix*—a Latin word referring to a lewd woman and sometimes used to refer to a woman who had sex with a woman.

- *hetairistriai*—women who are attracted to other women.

- *kinaidos*—a word for effeminate, a man "whose most salient feature was a supposedly *feminine* love of being sexually penetrated by other men."

- *lakkoproktoi*—a lewd and vulgar reference to anal penetration.

- *lesbiai*—a synonym referencing same-sex sexual relations between women.

- *paiderasste*—sexual behavior between males.

- *paiderastēs* or *paiderastïs*—lover of boys.

- *paidomanes*—a male mad for boys or boy-crazy.

- *paidophthoros*—a Greek word meaning corrupter of boys.

- *pathikos*—the passive penetrated partner in a male couple.

- *tribas*—the active partner in a female-female relationship, who takes the "male role."[23]

---

23. Thanks to my friends at GayChristian101.com for compiling this list.

If Paul was explicitly seeking to outrightly condemn homosexual relationships in any of his texts, he could have and would have used a more common word that his readers would have immediately understood. He doesn't do this, which makes it incredibly likely that he is not referring to homosexuality as it was and is most commonly understood.

The other word that Paul uses in the 1 Corinthians passage is the Greek word *malakoi*, which is a common Greek word that translates in modern vernacular as "effeminate men" or "boys." The most basic meaning of the word is literally "soft," and it's used to describe clothes, breezes, gourmet food, as well as men who are "soft" or "effeminate." When the word is used as a moral condemnation in the ancient world, it is most often used to suggest that someone is lazy, lacks courage, and is therefore feminine in disposition. In the ancient Greco-Roman world in particular, women were seen as lesser than men because they were literally soft and penetrable. Men were superior because they dominated, their bodies tended to be naturally stronger, and they penetrated, both with their penis in sexual encounters, but also as hunters in the fields and warriors on the battlefields.

Therefore, it becomes easy to understand why the Greco-Roman culture would think any man who allowed himself to be penetrated sexually by another man was willfully giving up his coveted masculinity, thus making himself *malakos* and becoming like a woman, which would have been a reason for him to be marginalized and despised in this hyper-patriarchal culture. In general, however, this is not the context that *malakos* is most often used in. Another common word, *kinaedos*, was the typical Greek word that literally meant a man who is the passive partner in a sexual relationship.

When *malakos* was describing a man, it was describing something about his fundamental nature as "weak or feminine." If that man was being penetrated sexually by another man (being a *kinaedos*), then it was also likely true that he would have been viewed as *malakos*. But being *malakos* does not necessarily mean the man has been sexually penetrated by another man. Again, the most common understanding of the word *malakos* in first-century

Greek was as a word used to shame men for being weak, effeminate, or cowardly. In this way, it could have been used equally for
homosexual and heterosexual men. There is virtually no debate
among reputable scholars that *malakos* simply meant "effeminate"
or "young boy" in the patriarchal Greco-Roman culture, and likely
did not explicitly refer to consensual same-sex sexual relationships, but to the temple priests to the young boys who were forced
into pederastic sexual encounters and effeminate men.

Paul, a Man of His Times

Even though I think our modern heterosexist reading of these
texts is wrong and leads us to unfaithful conclusions, I have no
problem conceding the fact that I believe Paul, a first-century Jewish teacher, would likely have been homophobic and condemning
of same-sex relationships, even modern ones. This is because Paul,
like every other historical figure, was a man of his time, and his
culture and religion were deeply rooted in patriarchy, which as we
have seen, led him and most other people in his culture to view
anything feminine as less than ideal.

It also bears restating that Paul and much of the early church
took a radical view of sex that almost no Christians accept today—
they believed all sexual passions outside of procreative ones, including heterosexual, homosexual, or otherwise, were flawed and
potentially dangerous to the life of the Christian. Paul makes it
clear that celibacy and abstinence are the preferred path for Christians in his day. One of the primary drivers of this understanding
of sexuality was because Paul and the early Christians believed that
Jesus was literally coming back to earth in their lifetime and that
they should devote their full passion and attention to preparing
themselves and the world for the reign of Christ. When Paul speaks
of marriage in 1 Corinthians 7:9, he echoes this idea, writing: "If
you cannot control yourselves and your passions, you should get
married. For it is better to be married than to burn with passion."

One can feel Paul's reluctance to endorse marriage and even
sense judgmental glare at those who simply can't control their

sexual passions, for in the sexual ethic of the Greco-Roman culture, to be enflamed with sexual passion was to be weak. There is part of this that should be regarded as true even today—if we cannot control and rule over our passions, sexual or otherwise, they can become consuming and destructive to our health and wellbeing. But in Paul's writing, marriage was seen as the best and the only way for individuals who could not completely overcome their sexual passion and devote their energy to building the kingdom of God to express those flaming passions in a non-sinful manner. Again, to need to be in a marriage relationship instead of reigning in your sexual passions was the less than ideal path by most Christians. The early Christian theologian Saint Jerome advocated for all Christians to remain virgins and dedicate themselves to Christ. In fact, his view of virginity and sexual purity was so strict that he taught even thinking sexual thoughts could cause you to "lose" the purity of your virginity. In a letter to a young virgin, he writes:

> Virginity may be lost with a thought. Such are evil virgins, virgins in the flesh, not in the spirit.[24]

If sex was to be used at all, it was to have procreative purposes, and once offspring were produced, sexual behavior was meant to stop in order to keep the marriage relationship pure. The philosophy of the early church all the way up through Augustine was heavily influenced by the renowned philosopher Plato's teaching that untamed sexual desire was a sign of weakness and ultimately rebellion towards God. Heterosexual sex and marriage as a whole were generally not as desirable in much of the ancient world as it becomes in later periods of history, and the same would have been true about same-sex relationships in general as well.

THE ORDERING OF CREATION

The final traditionalist scripture that is often cited in the case against LGBT+ inclusion comes from the creation passage in the Book of Genesis. The argument is traditionally articulated by

24 Jerome, Letter XXII.5.

saying that Genesis, when viewed as literal history, describes how God ordered creation and put male and female in a complementary, covenanted relationship with one another. It is this fundamental relationship that the sacrament of marriage is based upon, and therefore, any deviation from this opposite-sex covenant is a distortion of God's design in creation. Traditionalists will often cite Jesus' response to a question about marriage in Mark 10:8 where he quotes from the Genesis passage saying: "For this reason, a man will leave his father and mother and be united to his wife, and the two will become one flesh."

Jesus' affirmation of this male and female relationship is seen as his own reassertion of the idea that marriage is only for the male and female relationship, and thus, his words are a condemnation of same-sex marriage and relationships. While this argument has become arguably the most prominent in traditionalist circles, I have never found it very convincing for a number of key reasons.

First, this interpretation requires us to view the creation story in Genesis 2 as a literal historical account of how God created humanity and therefore an enduring record of the beginning of the covenant of marriage. Most modern biblical scholars (including evangelical scholars) would agree that Genesis 2 is *not* offering a historical account (in any sense that we would recognize as historical) and is clearly a cultural creation narrative that mirrored many other similar narratives in the ancient world. Genesis 2 might be best thought of as myth (remembering that myth can convey truth and divine revelation just as an historical text can). To take Genesis literally is to misunderstand its literary form as religious myth and seeks to make the myth do what it was never intended to. By making Adam and Eve literal historical figures whose relationship *literally* is the foundation of marriage is simply a historically and scientifically, indefensible position.

The Genesis 2 creation account is better understood as a metaphor for the creation of the world and of human relationships. It begins with a God who creates a human (not necessarily gendered) in God's own image. God then realizes that it is not good for the human to be alone—meaning without someone like him. Of course, the human isn't truly *alone*—he's surrounded by God and the animals. But after Adam spends time naming and examining and naming each animal, apparently checking each to see if they would be a relationally fit for him, the Scriptures says, "But a helper perfect for him was nowhere to be found."[25] God saw that animals were not sufficient for the human, and that the human needed *another human* to relate to and form a relationship with, which is why God creates a second human out of the first and names her "Eve." At the end of the second chapter of Genesis, we see a differentiation of the gender identity of Adam and Eve as male and female, and they enter into a covenantal relationship to support one another and procreate through what would later be called "marriage." What's important to note here is that gender identity does not seem to be central to this relational equation— what makes Eve suitable for Adam is that she is "bone from [his] bones and flesh from [his] flesh,"[26] she is a human just as he is. It was the *similarities* between Adam and Eve that make this relation- ship suitable and the incongruence between Adam and the rest of the animals that made those relationships unsuitable. It is the *humanity* of Eve that is important, not her gender identity.

When Jesus refers back to this creation narrative when asked about divorce in Mark 10:2–12, it is not to highlight the male and female differentiation, but rather to reemphasize the sacredness of covenant commitment in human relationships. By quoting from Genesis, he is signaling to the Pharisee's that the marriage covenant has its foundation in the very ordering of creation, prior to the laws of Moses, which is what the Pharisee's are relying on to try to stump Jesus' with their question on divorce. Jesus then quotes from Gen- esis 2:24 to solidify his case that the fundamental ordering of human relationships from the beginning was covenant commitment.[27] To make Jesus' teaching about sex differentiation misses the entire con- text of his question and misunderstands the Genesis narrative—nei-

25. Genesis 2:20b.

26. Genesis 2:23.

27 Keen, "Scripture, Ethics, and the Possibility of Same-Sex Relationships," 32.

ther were ever about the gender or sex of the people involved, rather, it was about whether the covenant that this hypothetical couple had entered into could or should be broken. Jesus' answer is simple: no, except in cases of unfaithfulness between the partners.

The key to the ordering of relationships in both Genesis and then in Jesus' reciting of those scriptures in the Gospel of Mark is covenant commitment between humans. Any relationship centered on a consensual commitment to sacrificial love for the good of another is a holy relationship, and any attempt to break that commitment is seen as less than God's desire for humanity. The covenanted relationship is the foundation of human society, in the Judeo-Christian worldview, and it dates back to the very beginning of humanity's time on the earth and has carried humans forward to the present day. Covenant relationships are vital to human flourishing—whether romantic or platonic, whether between the opposite sex or the same sex.

Conclusion

As we can clearly see, the six so-called "clobber" passages in Scripture that reference same-sex sexual behavior have nothing to do with same-sex relationships or queer sexual orientations, but are most often prohibitions of exploitative behavior by non-Judeo-Christian cultures. At the same time, as I said in the beginning of this chapter, I don't think we can firmly conclude that the authors of the biblical texts would *support* LGBT+ relationships if they were transported to our modern culture. Because of their hyper-patriarchal worldview, which we will explore in depth later, they condemn such relationships like many non-affirming Christians do today. However, we shall soon see why embracing this patriarchal lens is contrary to the thrust and ethical trajectory of Scripture as a whole.

3

The Redemptive Trajectory
Heeding the Spirit's Call towards Inclusion

The foundational beliefs of the Christian faith are often summarized in what the writers of the New Testament call "the
gospel." This word gospel comes from the Greek *euangelion*, which
literally means, "good news." This word "gospel" appears dozens of
times throughout the New Testament, and is used to refer to the
message that Jesus himself came to proclaim and embody, contain-
ing the keys to salvation for humankind. To begin thinking about
the metanarrative of Christian theology, there is no more essential
place to start than here. Throughout the biblical texts themselves
and Christian theology through the ages there is much variance
in what exactly the message of the gospel is. For our purposes, I
will root my understanding in the definition that the writer of The
Gospel of Mark has Jesus speaking, because many biblical scholars agree that Mark's Gospel contains some of the most reliable
quotes from Jesus, based on earlier source texts.[1] In chapter 1 of
the Gospel, the author of Mark says:

1. For more on the Marcan Priority theory, see Goodacre, *The Synoptic Problem*, 20–23.

> Jesus came into Galilee announcing God's good news,
> saying: "Now is the time! Here comes God's Kingdom!
> Change your hearts and lives, and trust this good news![2]

According to this passage, the "good news" that Jesus
preached was quite concise and simple: it is the announcement
that the kingdom of God was coming and an invitation to change
our hearts and lives to trust in the emerging reality of that kingdom. Throughout of the rest of Jesus' teachings as portrayed in
the Synoptic Gospels, he repeats this message about the arrival of
the kingdom of God over and over again. The gospel according to
Jesus is about this new reality he called the kingdom of God, and
therefore, this must be the foundation of all Christian theology
and practice.

The Ever-Expanding Kingdom of God

What, then, is the kingdom of God, and what impact might it
have on our understanding of the inclusion of sexual and gender
minorities in the life of the church? To answer this question, we
turn to the words of the apostle Paul in his Epistle of the Romans,
where he writes: "For the kingdom of God is . . . justice, and peace,
and joy in the Holy Spirit."[3] In this statement, Paul, writing to the
church at Rome in the midst of great conflict over how to observe
Jewish laws and customs, suggests that the kingdom of God is not
some far-off, supernatural reality, but rather a Spirit-led movement
of justice, peace, and joy, realities that should be experienced in the
life of the church and in the world here and now.

Theologian Jürgen Moltmann builds on Paul's definition,
suggesting that the kingdom of God is a present, tangible reality,
brought and demonstrated in the person of Jesus himself, as well
as a spiritual reality, described as an ever-deepening union with
God. Moltmann writes:

2. Mark 1:14–15, CEB.
3. Romans 14:17.

[The] Kingdom of God—that means God is near and present and allows God's creatures to participate in God's attributes, in God's glory and beauty, in God's vivacity and God's goodness, because at the same time God participates in the attributes of God's creatures, in their finiteness, in their vulnerability, and in their morality. (1 John 4:6) . . .The church is not there for its own sake but rather for the "concern of Jesus." All inherent interest of the church itself . . . must be subordinated to the interests of the Kingdom of God. . . . The divine mission of the church consists [of] bringing the oppressed their freedom, the humiliated their human dignity, and those without rights their rights. . . . [We must] participate in the Kingdom of God and today let something from the rebirth of all things become visible which Christ will complete on his day.[4]

Moltmann, echoing the words of both Paul and Jesus, furthers our understanding that the kingdom of God must be acknowledged to be a present and growing reality of union with God, resulting in the expansion of justice, peace, and equity for all of God's creatures. According to Jesus, in his many parables about the kingdom of God, it is both a present reality and one that continues to grow and progress. When Jesus speaks of the kingdom, he likens it to leaven in dough[5] and a seed planted in a field.[6] The imagery used here is one of gradual growth and expansion, requiring human effort to knead the dough and cultivate the seeds that are planted. Another way to understand this is to say that Jesus, in his life, planted the seeds of the kingdom. He demonstrated in his own actions what it looks like to live in step with the kingdom of God, or the world as God intends it to be. He then left it up to his disciples to cultivate the seeds so that the kingdom of God would grow and expand throughout the earth as the reality of justice and equity for all people over time.

---

4. Moltmann, "Jesus and the Kingdom of God," 15–16.
5. Matthew 13:33.
6. Matthew 13:31–32.

To be a disciple of Jesus is to be one who "changes your heart and life and trusts"[7] in the path that Jesus demonstrated. According to the teachings of the Gospels, this is what will bring ultimate wholeness to our world. But as we clearly see throughout the entire life of Jesus, his path is not an easy or convenient one to follow. It requires humility, sacrifice, and selflessness. It shouldn't be surprising to us, then, that a majority of what is sold as "Christianity" in our world has little to do with this message of liberation and equality for all people, but one that has been abstracted by theological musings and understood to be about a supernatural salvation in the afterlife, with little influence on the world we live in now.

A Kingdom for the Oppressed

If the message at the heart of Christianity is a message of an ever-expanding reality of justice and equality for those societies most marginalized and oppressed, then that must be the starting point for any conversation pertaining to inclusion in the church. As prominent black liberation theologian James Cone notes:

> Any view of the gospel that fails to understand the church as that community whose work and conscious-ness are defined by the community of the oppressed is not Christian and is thus heretical.[8]

In Cone's understanding, unless the message that is preached and embodied by Christian communities fully reflects the life and teaching of Jesus and his preferential option for the poor, marginalized, and oppressed of society, then it cannot be accepted as true Christianity.

This understanding of the gospel has roots in the teachings of Jesus himself and has been a common understanding throughout Christian history. From the early patristic writings[9] through the

7. Mark 1:15.

8. Cone, *God of the Oppressed*, 37.

9. J. Cameron Carter draws extensively on early Christian sources for liberation in his groundbreaking book *Race: A Theological Account*.

abolitionist movements of the 1700s, the liberationist movement of the early 1900s,[10] and the feminist movements of mid-1900s,[11] the idea that the message of Jesus was directed to society's most oppressed groups has undergirded Christian teaching for two thousand years. Any understanding of Christianity that lacks this liberationist undergirding, then, is failing to interpret the gospel through the lens of Jesus and the writings of the Gospels, which cast Christ's entire mission and ministry in a liberationist light.

Reading the Bible Like Jesus

One major reoccurring theme in the Synoptic Gospels is that Jesus continually finds himself battling with the religious leaders of his day over his seeming disregard for the religious dogma derived from the Hebrew Bible. Over a dozen times throughout the written accounts,[12] the Pharisee's and Sadducees are found confronting Jesus for his blatant disregard for biblical law or religious custom. Jesus, however, seems to take great delight in frustrating these religious leaders, offering new interpretations and further progressions on the laws of old. For instance, the Gospel of Matthew records a long series of teachings in which Jesus directly quotes from the Hebrew Bible and then directly contradicts the commandment and raises the ethical standard. He begins his teaching by saying, "Do not think that I have come to abolish the Law, but to fulfill it."[13] The word *plērōsai*, which is translated "fulfill" in many Bible translations of this verse, can also be translated as "complete." I believe that this translation helps us understand what Jesus is trying to communicate in this teaching.

Progressive revelation is the belief that God reveals more and more truth over time, as humanity is able to receive and adopt the

10. See the work of Gustavo Gutiérrez, Jon Sobrino, James Cone.

11. See the work of Marie Maugeret, Elisabeth Schüssler Fiorenza, Cathrine Keller.

12. For a sampling of these confrontations, see Matthew 15:1; 16:1–6; 23:1–4; Luke 11:37; 14:3.

13. Matthew 5:17.

"fullness of truth." In the Christian tradition, Jesus is understood to be the embodiment of the fullness of truth, the example of what a life live in accordance with the will of God looks like. As the writer of the Epistle to the Hebrews says, "In the past, God spoke through the prophets to our ancestors in many times and many ways. In these final days, though, he has spoken to us through his Son."[14] Jesus is seen as the supreme revelation of God to earth, in whom "the fullness of God was pleased to dwell."[15] His words, then, are seen to be the completion and truest embodiment of many of the Hebrew Bible's commands, which were only partially or incompletely revealed.

In Matthew 5, we witness Jesus building upon laws from the Hebrew Bible and bring them to a more complete and holistic ethical standard. For instance, he says:

> You have heard that it was said, "An eye for an eye and a tooth for a tooth." But I say to you that you must not oppose those who hurt you. If people slap you on your right cheek, you must turn the left cheek to them as well.[16]

Jesus quotes directly from Exodus 21:24, and then significantly amends the commandment, raising the ethical standard. Now, his disciples aren't permitted to retaliate, but are commanded to embrace non-violent resistance as the norm. The ethic has been altered, the standard has been raised. Jesus renders the old law inadequate in light of his new law, rooted in unconditional love. Jesus does this six times over the course of Matthew 5, each time taking a biblical commandment and amending it to be more ethical and just.

Not only does Jesus consistently expand the teaching of Scripture to align with a higher ethical standard, but he consistently reinterprets ancient commands in a more inclusive manner. For instance, when Jesus is asked what the greatest commandment is in the Gospel of Mark 12, he replies:

14. Hebrews 1:1–2.
15. Colossians 1:19.
16. Matthew 5:38–39.

The first is, "Hear, O Israel: the Lord our God, the Lord is one; you shall love the Lord your God with all your heart, and with all your soul, and with all your mind, and with all you strength." The second is this, "You shall love your neighbor as yourself." There is no other commandment greater than these.[17]

In the Jewish consciousness of Jesus day, the correct answer to the question was what Jesus said first, known as the *Shema*, the traditional saying from Deuteronomy that is at the heart of the Jewish religion: there is but one God, and that God alone is worthy of our worship. But to this highest and holiest command, Jesus adds "love your neighbor as yourself," which virtually no Rabbi in the first century would have placed anywhere near the importance of this central Jewish creed. In fact, the only place the phrase "love your neighbor as yourself" appears in the Hebrew Bible is in an obscure passage in Leviticus 19:17–18 where it is couched in a series of commands for the Hebrew people to love and protect *themselves* and *their families*. Jesus removes this obscure command from it's original context and greatly expands its meaning. When Jesus applies this commandment he says that it means to love *every human* as yourself, including your *enemy*, a vastly different command from the original context, which advocated that the faithful Hebrew person was to love their fellow Jew as themselves.[18] In this teaching, Jesus fundamentally links *loving your human neighbor* with *loving God*, and illustrates this inclusive ethic in story after story that he tells to his disciples, and in the inclusive table fellowship he engages in throughout his ministry. As Palestinian theologian Naim Stifan Ateek notes, "Jesus forever shattered any narrow and exclusive meaning and interpretation of the love of neighbor."[19]

Jesus clearly has no problem amending Scripture to be more ethical and inclusive, and therefore it cannot be argued that Jesus

17. Mark 12:28–34.

18. Brownfeld, "It Is Time to Confront the Exclusionary Ethnocentrism in Jewish Sacred Literature," 10.

19. Ateek, *A Palestinian Theology of Liberation*, 87.

was working from a paradigm even remotely similar to that of modern of biblical inerrancy. For Jesus, the Bible was a living text, always evolving and always being brought nearer to "completion." This makes sense when one realizes that *most* of the Rabbis of old viewed the Scriptures as texts to be reinterpreted, revised, and reconfigured based on the current era and context that they found themselves in. This tradition was known as midrash, which is described by Hebrew literature scholar Dr. David Stern in the following way:

> [Midrash is] a specific name for the activity of biblical interpretation as practiced by the Rabbis of the land of Israel in the first five centuries of the common era. . . . By the end of the biblical period, the locus for [the search for God's will] appears to have settled on the text of the Torah where, it was now believed, God's will for the present moment was to be found.[20]

In other words, midrash was a traditional rabbinical method, which relied upon the written text of the Torah to find wisdom and guidance for the present moment. This resulted in texts being taken out of their original context (an act considered *the* chief hermeneutical "sin" among evangelical theologians) and applied to situations in which the original author could never have even considered. In the rabbinical tradition, there were two forms of midrashic interpretation: midrash halacha, which was a form of interpretation that centered on explaining and applying the legal commands of the Torah to contemporary life; midrash aggadah, on the other hand, sought to reinterpret stories and teachings from Scripture into more accessible teachings that applied to the present context.[21] It is from this second form of midrash that many of the non-biblical Jewish parables and stories emerge that hold similar weight to that of Scripture because the stories are meant to repackage and reincarnate the teaching of Scripture for average laypeople to understand.

---

20. Berlin and Stern, *Jewish Study Bible*, 1864
21. Silberman and Dimitrovsky, "Talmud and Midrash."

It is from the hermeneutical practice of midrash in both forms that the Talmud emerges, a text considered sacred by the Jewish religion for its clarification and documentation of the oral teachings and traditions surrounding the interpretation of the Bible. The Talmud is the key text relied on by Jewish interpreters of Scripture to help understand the application of biblical teachings in a modern context. Midrash became increasingly important in the era after the destruction of the Second Temple in 70 C.E. when the Rabbis needed to reinterpret the Jewish faith for a world that was not dependent on a temple. The Jewish leaders believed that God had given the Torah to them to be an eternally enduring book with endless interpretations for every age. Prominent Scholar of Judaism Dr. Barry Holtz explains:

> Torah, to the rabbis, was an eternally relevant book because it was written (dictated, inspired—it doesn't matter) by a perfect Author, an Author who intended it to be eternal. . . . The rabbis could not help but believe that this wondrous and sacred text, the Torah, was intended for all Jews and for all times. Surely, God could foresee the need for new interpretations; all interpretations, therefore, are already in the Torah text. Thus, we have the idea mentioned previously: on Mount Sinai God gave not only the Written Torah that we know, but the Oral Torah, the interpretations of Jews down through time.[22]

This approach to Scripture has made Judaism an enduring and adaptable faith, molding to the changing world around it and reapplying the wisdom of the past to the new knowledge of the present era. This is the tradition that Jesus was birthed into and from which the church was founded. Scripture, in this context, is not viewed as a static text with a single meaning for all time, but a constantly changing and evolving text that speaks new wisdom to new times. The Midrashic approach views Scripture as a channel through which the Spirit of God could illumine old wisdom for new circumstance, resulting in new interpretations and new ideas from the biblical text. As we can see, throughout history, the

22. Holtz, "Back to the Sources: Reading the Classic Jewish Texts," 185.

biblical texts have always been seen as "living and active"[23] and not static and unchanging. This is how Jesus viewed the texts himself, bringing many of the existing ethical interpretations of laws from the Hebrew Bible to their completion through consideration of those on the margins. To many, this looked like transgression of the law, and indeed, it was. But in transgressing one version of the law, Jesus revealed a higher standard for his disciples to live by. Biblical scholar Cheryl Anderson notes that: "Jesus violated [traditional] standards to reincorporate those who had been excluded. . . . [T]he inclusive table fellowship of Jesus stands in stark contrast to the exclusive table fellowship of the Pharisees."[24]

Jesus, as a faithful Jew, felt free to reinterpret and expand upon the biblical texts in order to strain towards inclusion and equality. However, the fundamentalists in his day, as in ours, were uncomfortable with the freedom Jesus expressed in his engagement with the biblical texts, and therefore condemned him as unfaithful time and time again. Anytime a religious tradition is reinterpreted to be more inclusive, the balance of power is always thrown off, which causes those with the most power to cling tighter to their way of seeing the tradition and to more viciously oppose those threatening their power with more just and generous interpretations of the text.

The Continuing Revelation of the Holy Spirit

Furthermore, Jesus makes it clear that God's revelatory work will not cease with him. Indeed, he tells his disciples that the Holy Spirit would continue its revelatory work indefinitely. Jesus says to his disciples, "I still have much to tell you, but you cannot yet bear to hear it. However, when the Spirit of truth comes, [it] will guide you into all the truth."[25] In other words, as Jesus is looking towards his nearing death, he tells the disciples that there is much more that he desires for them to know, but doesn't believe they

---

23. Hebrews 4:12.

24. Anderson, *Ancient Laws and Contemporary Controversies*, 92.

25. John 16:12–13.

are able to bear it at the present time. Most Christian traditions hold the doctrine of progressive revelation to be true—Roman Catholic, Orthodox, and Pentecostal Christians, yet those from the Reformed traditions have tended to reject this notion in favor of holding to one interpretation of Scripture as authoritative above all others, in stark contrast to the majority Christian and Jewish tradition. Jesus demostrated a foundational belief that God has (and will) reveal truth progressively, over time, as humanity is able to "bear" or comprehend it. As evangelical theologian Dr. Vern Poythress writes, describing progressive revelation: "God did not say everything at once. The earlier communications take into account the limitations in the understanding of people at earlier times. The later communications build on the earlier."[26]

God is still speaking. Though the biblical canon may be closed as a matter of tradition, the ongoing revelatory work of God clearly continues to unfold throughout human history, leading society towards higher ethical ideals of inclusion, equality, and wholeness. This reality has been and is currently experienced by followers of Christ throughout the ages and is completely aligned with the teachings and expectations of Jesus. If we are to be faithful to God in our present age, we must pay close attention to the nudges of the Spirit, gently calling us to step beyond our beliefs and traditions to widen the gates of the kingdom of God.

Paul's Radically Inclusive Gospel

One of the fiercest debate among the early followers of Christ was whether or not gentiles should be included in the fledgling Christian community. Because Jesus was Jewish and primarily ministered to Jewish people (although there are a few notable exceptions), the early disciples apparently leaned towards understanding that the gospel that Jesus proclaimed was primarily intended for a Jewish audience, to the exclusion of gentiles. After Jesus' ascension, the apostles begin forming new communities that meet regularly to

26. Lillback, Poythress, Duguid, Beale, and Gaffin, *Seeing Christ in All of Scripture*, 10.

worship, pray, and live in radical communion with one another in the way of Jesus. Eventually the example of these believers attracts the attention of a Pharisee named Saul who is incensed at this new messianic communities' lack of respect for the laws and traditions of the Jewish faith and spends much time and energy persecuting and even killing Christians.

After a miraculous conversion experience, Saul—also known as Paul—takes his place among the leaders of the new Christian movement, adopting the title and role of apostle. Very quickly, Paul comes into conflict with the bona fide leader of the church, the apostle Peter, over whether or not obeying the ritual laws of Judaism was necessary for Christians and if non-Jewish people could become a part of the church. Paul begins preaching that in Christ the Jewish law had found it's fulfillment, and therefore gentile Christians were free from the obligations of the law. Along with this new freedom was the invitation of all people—Jew and gentile alike—to respond to the story of Jesus by becoming active participants in the community of faith. Paul urges the council of apostles to allow him to go into the world and tell the gentiles about Jesus and establish Christian churches throughout the pagan world. This impulse was greeted at first with great skepticism, but eventually the apostles blessed Paul and sent him to spread the message of Jesus far and wide.

In the Book of Romans, Paul begins writing to the emerging (primarily) gentile Christian community in the midst of the city of Rome, the capital of the Empire. Paul wanted to clarify the nature of gospel, the story of Jesus and the invitation to all people to follow in his path. We must make a distinction between the gospel that Jesus himself proclaimed and the gospel message proclaimed by Paul and the early church. The former is what *Jesus himself* proclaimed about the coming of God's Kingdom, while the gospel message of Paul and others centered on the implications of Jesus' life for the world. According to Paul, his gospel was to communicate the story of how Jesus had come to reveal God's kingdom and righteousness and to draw all of humanity into participation within it.

Paul writes this in Romans 16:25: "Now to him who is able to establish you according to my gospel and the preaching of Jesus Christ." Notice the distinction—Paul's gospel and the preaching of Jesus Christ: two separate messages that support each other and lay a foundation for the radical inclusion that has been revealed as the heart of God's plan for humanity. The movement Jesus gave birth to is not for one religion, one ethnicity, or one class. According to the ministry of Paul, God is inviting the entire world to taste of redemption and reconciliation, a fundamental shift from the initial posture of the early Christians.

Paul goes on to clearly identify what exactly "his gospel" entails. In Romans 3:5–6, Paul writes:

> God showed me his secret plan. . . . Earlier generations didn't know this hidden plan that God has now revealed to his holy apostles and prophets through the Spirit. The plan is that the gentiles would be coheirs and parts of the same body, and that they would share with the Jews in the promises of God in Christ Jesus through the gospel.

Paul says that *his* gospel has been kept a secret, a mystery, and that through Christ and through Paul, God has chosen to reveal God's truest heart, that *all* the nations would join in the kingdom through obedience of faith and become members of the same spiritual body as the Jewish people and partakers in the same promises that God had made to the people of Israel. This is indeed good news and an important development in Christian history. If it wasn't for this revelation, the message of God's inclusive embrace through Jesus would have never been proclaimed to the gentile world and would have limited the scope and impact of Jesus on the world.[27]

Paul's eyes were opened to see that God's long plan of redemption was not limited to one singular group of people, but for the redemption of the whole world. This wasn't a new idea—the Hebrew scriptures speak of God's desire to redeem all nations—but

27. Special thanks to my friend Pastor Mark DeYmaz who first opened my eyes to the distinction between Paul's gospel and Jesus' teaching. You can read more about this distinction in his book *Disruption*.

in the early Christian community, most of the apostles seem to have functioned in an exclusionary manner towards non-Jewish people. But when Paul got a glimpse of what God was planning to do through Jesus, he joyfully and zealously shared the story of Christ with anyone and everyone who would listen, and the Spirit of God moved in power to bring gentiles into the fold. This movement from a narrow and exclusive understanding of redemption to a broader, more inclusive understanding is a consistent theme throughout the course of the biblical canon. The expansiveness of God's work begin with one person in the Garden of Eden and ends with every nation tribe and tongue in the Book of Revelation—the trajectory of history, seen through the Judeo-Christian lens, is always towards inclusion and expansion, and that truth makes the gospel of Jesus Christ truly good news of great joy for absolutely all people.[28]

28. Luke 2:10.

4

Forward towards Inclusion
Exploring Inclusive Interpretation

When one examines the way that Jesus and the early apostles used Scripture, we begin to see a clear trajectory towards higher ethical standards and a more inclusive vision for the kingdom of God. In 2001, evangelical theologian William Webb published a groundbreaking book[1] in which he posited a hermeneutical lens for interpreting Scripture that he called "the redemptive-movement hermeneutic." This hermeneutic traced the redemptive trajectory of ethics from the Hebrew Bible to the New Testament, showing that the ethical consciousness of society continually grew, albeit slowly, towards a more inclusive and equal posture for all people. Webb's hermeneutic argued that faithful Christians are called to move beyond the static words of Scripture, taking the "spirit" of the words and applying them to our modern contexts to help us determine the faithful response to our ethical questions. Webb writes:

> Scripture does not present a "finalized ethic" in every area of human relationship[;] . . . to stop where the Bible stops (with its isolated words) ultimately fails to reapply

1. Webb, *Slaves, Women & Homosexuals*.

49

> the redemptive spirit of the text as it spoke to the original
> audience. It fails to see that further reformation is pos-
> sible. . . . While Scripture had a positive influence in its
> times, we should take that redemptive spirit and move to
> an even better, more fully realized ethic today.[2]

Webb's argument opens the door for continued societal re-
form, based on the spirit of the biblical texts, rather than the static
words themselves. And while Webb's "redemptive-movement
hermeneutic" was groundbreaking for the evangelical world in
2001, it is hardly a new idea or concept. Instead, it has been clearly
demonstrated in the field of biblical interpretation[3] and indeed in
the biblical texts themselves for thousands of years. As we noted
earlier, feminist and liberationist theologians have relied on ethical
trajectories in Scripture and the cultural context of the writer as
the interpretive key to unlock the liberating power of the biblical
text. Feminist theologian Carol Lakey Hess notes:

> [Biblical] texts . . . reflect the prevailing cultural ethos[;]
> . . . we must use this to recognize that the biblical writers
> were human persons immersed in—though not limited
> to—the language, mores, customs, and assumptions of
> their day. . . . Some texts both reflect and challenge the
> cultural assumptions[;] . . . by looking at what is new,
> rather than what is the same, sometimes we can see a
> trajectory towardss greater liberation.[4]

Here, Hess reflects the hermeneutical idea of a redemptive ethical trajectory that has been demonstrated throughout biblical
interpretation for thousands of years. As theologian Derek Flood
echoes: "The New Testament is not a final unchangeable eternal
ethic, but rather the 'first major concrete steps' from the dominant

---

2. Webb, *Slaves, Women & Homosexuals*, 247.

3. Similar theological arguments have been made by a wide array of theologians in the modern era such as J. R. Daniel Kirk, Megan DeFranza, Dale
Martin, and I. Howard Marshall.

4. Hess, *Caretakers of Our Common House*, 197–98.

religious and political narrative . . . towardss a better way rooted in compassion."[5]

Peter's Inclusive Vision

One biblical text where this redemptive trajectory is most clearly on display is in the Book of Acts, chapter 10, where the apostle Peter falls into a God-induced trance and is called to preach the gospel to the unclean gentiles for the first time. In this account, Peter sees a vision of a sheet coming out of heaven, holding a plethora of biblically "unclean" animals. As Peter observes the sheet with confusion, he hears the voice of God speak to him three times, saying "Rise up, kill, and eat." Peter, being a student of Scripture, argues with the voice of God, saying that he could not kill and eat these unclean animals because to do so would be a violation of the purity codes of Scripture. On the third go around, the voice of God responds to Peter saying, "Do not call unclean that which I have made clean." With that, Peter awakens from the trance and finds the servants of a Cornelius, a Roman Centurion, knocking on his door, requesting that he come and speak to Cornelius and his household about the gospel. Immediately, Peter realizes that this vision was not about unclean foods but unclean people, the gentiles. Peter reluctantly goes with the servants to Cornelius's house to preach the gospel to them. As Peter arrives, he says to Cornelius, "You yourselves know that it is unlawful for a Jew to associate with or to visit a gentile; but God has shown me that I should not call anyone profane or unclean."[6] As Peter preaches, we are told, "while Peter was still speaking, the Holy Spirit fell upon all who heard the word."[7] The Spirit falls upon the gentiles; an example of the Spirit of God doing something unexpected, and perhaps even "unbiblical" in the light of previous biblical revelation.

5. Flood, *Disarming Scripture*, 127.

6. Acts 10:28.

7. Acts 10:44.

Peters actions of entering a gentile's home and baptizing the entire household into the church without first requiring them to obey the purity laws of Scripture was seen by the apostles and elders in Jerusalem potential to be a grave violation of biblical law. While it's important to note that first-century Judaism itself was quite theologically diverse and many adherents would not have held to such an exclusionary or strict understanding of the Levitical law, for Peter and the apostles, their interpretation of the purity codes seem to have initially prevented them from sharing the gospel of Jesus with the gentiles. After hearing about Peter's actions, the council of apostles summoned Peter to Jerusalem to receive criticisms[8] for this apparent violation of Scripture. As Peter stands before the council, he recounts the entire situation, beginning with his vision to the baptism of Cornelius' house, and concludes saying, "If then God gave them the same gift that he gave us when we believed in the Lord Jesus Christ, who was I that I could hinder God?"[9] When the Apostolic Council heard this, we are told, "They praised God, saying, 'Then God has given even to the gentiles the repentance that leads to life.'"[10] Both Peter and the council are open and willing to change their long-held theological beliefs and practices to coincide with the experiential evidence of God's Spirit working among the gentiles. For these leaders, there is no deep biblical deliberation, but an acknowledgement that if God so desired to save the gentiles, then the apostles' only job was to celebrate and participate in the new thing that God was doing in their midst.

For decades, this story of the conversion of the gentiles has been a cornerstone for an inclusive theology, demonstrating both the redemptive trajectory of Scripture and the value of experience and testing the fruits. As queer theologian Patrick Cheng notes, the dissolution of clean and unclean as religious categories began with the life and ministry of Jesus himself in the ways that he interacted with and included some of the most "unholy" individuals in the

8. Acts 11:2.

9. Acts 11:17.

10. Acts 11:18.

cultural consciousness of his day,[11] and this trend clearly continues in the theological approach of the earliest apostles. Therefore, it can be logically deduced that when we observe the approach of Peter and the apostles in regard to the authority given to ongoing the revelatory work of the Holy Spirit and the role of experience, we are seeing a regular pattern of theological growth and evolution towards greater inclusivity. Cheryl Anderson writes:

> [B]iblical scholars are now advancing understandings of God and interpretations of the biblical text that are different from traditional ones. Yet they are different only because they reflect the political and economic realities of women, the poor, and the foreigner and consider the impact that traditional interpretations have on these groups. Although those who uphold the traditional Christian interpretations, today's Pharisees, vilify this contextual approach, it is exactly the kind of approach that Jesus used.[12]

In our contemporary era, it seems clear that the Spirit of God continues to call humanity forward towards the higher ethical standards, and this belief is accepted by a majority of contemporary Christians when they examine their theological and ethical beliefs about slavery, the treatment of women, the discipline of children, divorce, corporal punishment, and a wide array of other ethical issues in which modern Christian teaching is significantly more ethical than what is prescribed in the Scriptures.

Webb goes great lengths to demonstrate that while the New Testament is, for instance, the final revelation of Scripture, the ethical perspectives of the New Testament have by no means been taken to their fullest realization in the static words of Scripture itself.[13] As one explores how the abolitionists, for example, viewed the trajectory of Scripture, it becomes abundantly clear that it was their understanding of the *spirit* of the biblical texts—rather than the plain, literal reading of the text—that directed their theologi-

11. Cheng, Radical Love, 80.

12. Anderson, *Ancient Laws and Contemporary Controversies*, 87.

13. Webb, "The Limits of a Redemptive-Movement Hermeneutic," 330.

cal fight to end slavery in Britain and the United States and was a source of great critique from traditionalist, pro-slavery Christians.[14] The same approach must be faithfully applied as Christians grapple with the "clobber passages" that seem to condemn same-sex relationships.

Applying a Redemptive Hermeneutic to Sexuality

It can be argued that throughout the entire biblical canon, there is a trajectory that shows how the biblical authors' understanding of gender roles and sex evolved over time towards a more egalitarian approach. While examples of ethical regression are also present in the New Testament—for instance, when one looks at how the writers of the Pastoral Epistles seem to suggest that women do not hold an equal place in the church—by and large the direction of the ethical trajectories in the Bible points towards a more liberating and inclusive posture for all people. It is in these same trajectories that the keys for full inclusion for LGBT+ people into the life of the Church can be found. It is in these same trajectories that the keys for full inclusion for LGBT+ people into the life of the church can be found. As theologian J. R. Daniel Kirk notes:

> For the same reason that we cannot claim anymore that men are better than women, for the same reason that we do not hold to a biblical view of marriage in which a man owns his wife, for the same reason that we err in excluding women from leading as they are gifted by the Spirit, the ground has been cut out from the ancient framework that excluded the notion of same-sex intercourse.[15]

The ethical trajectories of the biblical texts generally point towards more inclusive ways of seeing and being in the world. And as we will see in the final section of this book, there is much evidence to suggest that the Holy Spirit is working in and through sexual and gender minorities to bring about redemption and renewal in

14. Noll, *The Civil War as a Theological Crisis*.
15. Kirk, "Trajectories towards Gay Inclusion?" n.p.

contemporary Christianity. It is this combination of biblical ethical trajectories and experience that should lead contemporary Christians on the same theological journey of Peter and the earliest apostles. If the Spirit of God moves among LGBT+ people, who are Christians to stand in the way of the work of God? One can almost hear the Spirit speaking once again to the church today, saying, "Do not call unclean that which I have made clean!"[16]

16. Acts 10:15.

5

Leveling the Ground
Deconstructing Patriarchy

As we examine the biblical trajectory towards inclusion, we can begin to see that the primary ethical progression of the biblical arc is away from the patriarchal system that dominated the ancient world towards a more truly egalitarian ordering of society. The aforementioned evangelical scholar who developed the "Redemptive Movement Hermeneutic," William Webb, argues that there is in fact an anti-patriarchal movement in Scripture when it comes to the status of women, but Webb goes great lengths to try to show why that same movement doesn't apply towards the liberating trajectory of Scripture in regard to same-sex relationships.

Daniel Kirk has written at length in response to William Webb's book, arguing that Webb fails to accurately understand the way in which the ancient patriarchal social codes were constructed. Kirk defines patriarchy as "shorthand for a whole web of relationships in which people who are thought to be inherently superior rule over those who are thought to be inherently inferior."[1]

Kirk explains that in the ancient Hebrew social codes and in Greco-Roman household codes, sexuality, gender roles, and

1. Kirk, "Trajectories towards Gay Inclusion?"

societal class were all tied together, making all three of these issues inextricably linked in any discussion of ethical trajectories regarding them. All of the ancient social and household codes were seeking to uphold the patriarchal ordering of society, forcing women, effeminate men, and those in lower social classes to submit to a patriarchal power structure in order to uphold society, and for men of the dominant culture and class to live into a culturally defined notion of "manhood." It should be noted that *none* of these definitions find their origin in Scripture or from the mouth of God, but rather, emerge as a result of how many of the earliest human societies began to order themselves.[2] Patriarchy emerges as an intentional social ordering in the Neolithic era as men assumed the dominant role in the sexual relationship, became the hunters in the hunter gatherer societies, and eventually began to look at women, animals, and land as aspects of their world that should be subject to their ownership.[3] These ideas are later encoded in many ancient religious and social texts as men sought to uphold their dominance and power over the world.

In a patriarchal social order, if any lower level of being sought to supplant the dominant man at the top of the ordering of society then the entire social fabric would be threatened. For example, if women sought to leave their role as homemakers to become the hunters or the leaders of their tribe, the tribal patriarchy itself would be threatened and thus all of the structures of society. Therefore, there was great incentive for the culturally dominant men to keep women, slaves, or colonized peoples, and non-conforming, effeminate men, under the weight of their power to maintain control and influence over the society.

One of the key reasons that homosexuality was so despised in the ancient world was because it threatened the patriarchal system by causing a man to surrender his "rightful" place in society and making him "act like a woman," which was seen as a fundamental distortion of the ordering of the patriarchal world. In a patriarchal

---

2. One could also reasonably argue that patriarchy is a rather unevolved view that prevents humanity from progressing to higher social ordering.

3. "The History of Patriarchy."

mindset, sex, gender, and social class are all fundamentally linked, and the culturally dominant man is seen as the ideal human being. Men are considered superior because they are physically strong, they dominate on the battlefield, and they are the ones who penetrate, sexually, with their penis. Any person who does not conform to this idealized version of manhood is therefore seen as lesser and *must* be dominated in order for these "superior" men to keep their rightful role as the rulers of the world. This is why in ancient household codes it was often fine for a master to use a slave for sexual gratification, but it was never okay for a slave to sexually penetrate the master—this would have threatened the social order.[4]

Because the Hebrew and Christian traditions emerge from cultures where patriarchy was the assumed ordering of society, it makes sense then that the patriarchal worldview is built into the biblical worldview and, therefore, so is the oppression of women, lower classes, and LGBT+ people. Any person that was seen as weak or divergent from the cultural norms was seen as of lesser dignity and value and the writers of Scripture were clearly happy to use their religious texts to justify the patriarchal worldview of their culture. For evidence of how prominent patriarchy and misogyny were in the ancient world, one needs only to look at any of the prominent philosophers from just about any era. For instance, in his famous work *On Flight and Findings*, the renowned Jewish philosopher Philo goes as far to declare: "For the feminine always falls short and is inferior to the masculine."[5]

But in the face of such an oppressive and broken system of social ordering, the Christian faith emerges with a radically countercultural perspective on how the world should be ordered. In the New Testament, we see in the person of Jesus a sometimes subtle but nonetheless powerful assault on the patriarchal ordering of his society. Throughout his ministry, Jesus scandalously transgresses patriarchal cultural norms by elevating the position of women, often treating them as equals, reclining at their tables, and allowing them to be disciples. Jesus' very behavior and social position

4. Kirk, "Trajectories Towards Gay Inclusion?"
5. Philo, On Flight and Findings, IX.52.

within the Roman Empire also would have caused him to be viewed as feminine when contrasted with the citizen-men of the Roman Empire, as Dianna Swancutt notes in her groundbreaking article *Sexing the Pauline Body of Christ,* "Jesus and his disciples . . . were girls by Roman gender standards."[6]

And while racism and slavery aren't completely condemned in the New Testament, most readers of Scripture would agree that there is a consistent trajectory away from the patriarchal norms towards the liberation and equality of people of all races, classes, and cultures, from the principles of the Hebrew Bible to the standards of the New Testament. After all, the apocalyptic vision at the end of the Bible shows us a beautiful scene where every nation stands together as equals before the throne of the Lamb, thus ending cultural division and classism. Daniel Kirk speaks to this apocalyptic vision saying:

> God has created a different kind of society. In this society we can be either male or female. Or eunuch. And these don't affect our standing or inheritance. We can be either Jew or Gentile. Or messianic Jew. And these don't affect our standing or inheritance. We can be either slave or free. Or debt slave to our credit card. And these don't affect our standing or inheritance.[7]

In the kingdom that God is creating through Christ, all of our socially constructed identities take a backseat to our primary identity as children of God. No matter what our gender, sexuality, or social class, God invites us to stand on equal footing at the throne of the Lamb. This message is abundantly clear throughout the ministry of Jesus and later in the writings of the New Testament.

But when it comes to homosexuality, it *is* true that it's less clear to the naked eye how the New Testament flips the script on the treatment of sexual minorities. As we engage this topic, it's important to remember the point that I've stated numerous times thus far: since sex, sexuality, and social class are fundamentally linked in the patriarchal worldview, if we see a trajectory of liberation

6. Swancutt, *Theology of Eros,* 84.

7. Kirk, "Eschatological Trajectory of Gay Inclusion."

regarding sex and social class, then *necessarily* there must also be a trajectory of liberation for sexual minorities. But I think an even stronger case can be made when we dig deeper into the ways that patriarchy manifested in the Greco-Roman world and begin understanding how this system impacted the life of Jesus himself.

Why Gay Sex Was Taboo in the Ancient World

We've already established that in a patriarchal worldview, males are believed to be superior because they are seen as dominators. The reason that homosexuality, in particular (lesbianism is rarely mentioned or condemned in ancient texts), was seen as deplorable is because it fundamentally threatened the patriarchal ordering of society and culture. For a biological male to allow himself to be penetrated by another male was to allow himself to be emasculated and thus, to give up his social power and position. It bears repeating again that in the Greco-Roman world, one's sex was fundamentally tied to one's role in a sexual relationship, the two *could not* be separated. Therefore, for a man to be penetrated was to give up his "manhood" and thus his position of power in culture.[8] Scholar Diana Swancutt explores this in depth saying:

> Ancients treated intercourse not as a function of sexual orientation but as a gendered enactment of sociopolitical status understood in terms of masculinity and femininity of the actor's actions, irrespective of the sex of their sex objects. Greek and Roman citizen-men were defined as active, masculine penetrators, and their sex objects (women, slaves, and youths) as the passive/feminine/penetrated.[9]

Jonathan Walters argues that in Roman consciousness, the very identity of being a man was tied to the reality that their bodies could not and would not be sexually penetrated.[10] The reason that

8. Swancutt, "Still before Sexuality."
9. Swancutt, *Theology of Eros*, 77.
10. Walters, "Invading the Roman Body," 29.

homosexual sex was deplorable was because a man would *make himself* one of the *malakoi*, or a "soft ones," by being penetrated, while another man would willingly participate in the emasculating of a fellow male. The act of man-on-man sex cannot be made sense of in a system of patriarchy, and this is why homophobia was so prevalent in the ancient world, and in the biblical texts.

Until one gets a firm grasp of how misogyny and patriarchy functioned in the Greco-Roman world (and most of the other ancient societies of the Near East), they will fail to see just how prevalent these forces are and how they have shaped Christian theology and practice for thousands of years. But we must remember that the customs of an ancient culture are *not* to be confused with the desires of God. Until we are able to challenge both ancient and modern cultural standards with the clear example and teaching of Jesus, we will remain promoting oppressive, culturally constructed systems that exclude and limit the extent to which the gospel can transform lives and the world.

Crucifixion as Emasculation

Another way that the patriarchy symbolically sought to manifest its power was through capital punishment via crucifixion. Crucifixion was feared by all in the Roman Empire and was seen as one of the most reprehensible ways to die, to be reserved for the very worst criminals and social outcasts. The famed Roman writer Cicero declares of crucifixion: "The very word 'cross' should be far removed not only from the person of a Roman citizen, but from his thought, his eyes, and his ears."[11]

In the Greco-Roman world, crucifixion was seen as the highest form of capital punishment, not only because it was so excruciatingly painful, but because it sought to shame the "criminal" through dramatic acts of sexual shame and emasculation. Remember, in the Greco-Roman mind, *any* form of piercing of the body was seen as emasculating and shameful. In the drama of

11. Cicero, Pro Rabirio Postumo, 5.16.

crucifixion, the whole patriarchal system was symbolically coming down upon men who posed a threat to society, not only by publicly murdering them, but also by *emasculating* them. Absolutely no other form of death would have been more shameful for a man in a hyper-patriarchal society. Biblical scholar David Tombs notes:

> Crucifixion in the ancient world appears to have carried a strongly sexual element and should be understood as a form of sexual abuse that involved sexual humiliation and sometimes sexual assault. Crucifixion was intended to be more than the ending of life; prior to actual death it sought to reduce the victim to something less than human in the eyes of society. Victims were crucified naked in what amounted to a ritualized form of public sexual humiliation. In a patriarchal society, where men competed against each other to display virility in terms of sexual power over others, the public display of the naked victim by the "victors" in front of onlookers and passers-by carried the message of sexual domination. The cross held up the victim for display as someone who had been—at least metaphorically—emasculated.[12]

In traditional Christian theology, we believe that Christ goes willingly to the cross to demonstrate the wickedness of humanity's disordered pursuit of power and injustice. Christians believe that the crucifixion is *the* act of liberation and salvation for the world. At the cross, the empire strips Jesus of his dignity and power and murders him because of the threat his counter-cultural social and spiritual vision posed to the powers of the day. At the cross, Jesus is dramatically beaten, stripped naked, humiliatingly marched through the center of Jerusalem, and hung high on the cross, nails piercing his hands and feet and a spear piercing the side. Why so much nudity? Why so much drama? Why so much piercing? Because the act of crucifixion was meant to be the highest form of shaming, the most fearful death possible, where an individual's fundamental dignity, power, and life itself was slowly, dramatically stripped from them in front of a cheering crowd of onlookers. This

---

12. Tombs, "Crucifixion, State Terror, and Sexual Abuse: Text and Context."

was the patriarchy at its most vicious. Scholar Dianne Swancutt emphasizes the emasculating humiliation of the crucifixion of Christ, saying:

> As a Galilean Jew the Romans crucified as a royal pre-tender, Jesus embodied everything the Roman man was not—dominated, penetrated, scourged, and humiliated. To Roman eyes, therefore, the crucified Jesus was not king of the Jews, but a barely-man whom Rome nailed as a queen.[13]

In the Greco-Roman mind, when Christ is crucified on the cross, he also becomes emasculated.[14] The cross is the ultimate expression of power for the patriarchal system, in its misogyny, xenophobia, and homophobia. And traditional Christian theology teaches us that Jesus faces that cross willingly as *the* act of salvation. He humbles himself, even to the point of fully and finally giving up his culturally constructed version masculinity, power, and privilege for the liberation of the world. As Jesus dies, mocked and shamed for all to see, the empire believes it has gained victory over his fledgling revolution. It believes that through this horrendous display of patriarchal power, it has clearly demonstrated why Caesar is Lord and Jesus is not. The empire believes it has not only shamed Jesus himself through the crucifixion, but by emasculating their leader, it has also shamed all of his disciples who had hoped in his revolution as well. Theologian Halvor Moxnes notes that immediately after Jesus is crucified, ancient historical records tell us that the emasculation Jesus faced was also understood to have

13. Swancutt, *Theology of Eros*, 84.

14. The Greek word used for an emasculated male is malakoi, a "soft" one, which is the word that is mistranslated in most English Bibles as homosexual. To be clear, I am not asserting that Jesus was a homosexual, rather, that if we take the misinterpretation of malakoi to mean homosexuals, as in most English Bibles, then we would have to say Jesus was homosexual, because that's how we've translated malakoi. What I'd argue is that we should seek a better translation in our English Bibles for the word malakoi and also come to understand how seeing malakoi as a sin is fundamentally tied to misogyny and patriarchy, which the New Testament seeks to deconstruct.

"passed on" to his followers, who became mocked throughout the empire as "eunuchs."[15]

But then, in the Christian story, the resurrection happens. Perhaps the resurrection should be seen as the ultimate *subversion* of the oppressive patriarchal system. In Jesus' rising to life again after being murdered by the empire, he is proving that the revolution he began was more powerful than even the most powerful systems of oppression in our world. When Jesus rises from the dead, it is the ultimate declaration that neither the empire nor the patriarchy would have the last word. The previously emasculated and crucified Jesus rises and is declared by his followers to be the *Son of God*, the title of ultimate power limited to the Caesar himself, turning the whole idea of patriarchal power on its head.

The community of disciples organize themselves around the image of this crucified Messiah and even begin to reclaim the symbol of the cross—a symbol meant to strike terror in the heart of all who see it—using it as a subversive symbol of liberation. The patriarchy had been broken by the power of radical love and inclusion, and the crucified Savior was now the image of ultimate victory and strength.

In all of the resurrection narratives, the writers are clear to indicate that the risen Christ still bears the marks of his crucifixion. Even in his renewed life, his hands and feet bear scars of the traumatic abuse he was unjustly subjected to. In fact, as far as we can tell, for the rest of the New Testament, even to the apocalyptic visions of Revelation, Jesus *never loses* his wounds. *He remains scarred, he remains pierced.* He is *forever* marked by this symbol of emasculation, and he becomes the image of what redeemed masculinity—or rather, *true humanity*—should look like. As scholar Chris Frilingos suggests,[16] the image of the Lamb of God in Revelation stands in a unique tension as both a feminine and masculine image, suggesting the resurrected Christ eternally embodies the complex array of gender identities reflected in humanity. The resurrected Lamb ultimately shows that the oppressive system of

15. Moxnes, *Putting Jesus in His Place*, 72–90.
16. Frilingos, Sexing the Lamb.

patriarchy only has the potential to bring death, but the path of radical inclusion and embrace is what brings about the new world that God desires to create—one of equity and justice.

Despite this powerful imagery at the heart of the Christian narrative, many Christians have largely reverted back to the patriarchal way of seeing and being in the world—because nobody wants an effeminate Savior, especially in a patriarchal, dominator-centered culture like the modern Western world. When Christianity was eventually declared the official religion of the patriarchal Roman Empire, I believe that Jesus' embodiment of liberation from patriarchy became diluted in mainstream Christianity. What was expressed as "official" Christianity by those in power became a tool to uphold oppressive systems and create new systems to amass power and wealth.

This is also why in our modern day, most evangelical Christians have been taught not to gaze upon and long for our crucified Savior, but to hope for a second coming, when Jesus will appear, it is said, not as the Lamb of God but as the *warrior king* who will make battle, shed blood, and once again become the ultimate image of domination and patriarchy. Instead of the subversive image of Jesus revealed in the Gospel accounts—the one who overcomes oppression through declaring the outsiders "insiders," through challenging the religious and political systems of his day at every turn, through declaring forgiveness even to his murderers—evangelicals have been taught to desire a Jesus who *kills* their enemies, supports their empires, justifies their abuse, and oppresses everyone who doesn't believe or look like them. *This* is what has been taught in so much of Christianity throughout history up to our modern era. And this message is the *fundamental antithesis* of the message and example of the cross.

The Message of the Cross and Sexual Abuse[17]

In our modern era, the evil of patriarchy has also asserted itself in the church in many disturbing ways, not the least of which is through the prevalence of sexual abuse. When our theology supports a patriarchal way of seeing and being in the world, declaring that it is God who has ordered creation in this way, it becomes acceptable for men to assert their dominance in any way possible, including through sexual abuse.

While most Christians would never outrightly seek to justify sexual abuse, we have seen a staggering amount of sexual abuse that has been ignored, hidden, or justified in the church. Tragic stories have been documented online under the hashtag #ChurchToo[18] of church leaders engaging in or justifying sexual abuse as a means of protecting their platforms, using overtly patriarchal theology to do so. If women, queer people, and people of lower social classes are seen as of less worth or power than dominant men, then the moral outrage at their abuse is significantly lessened. It becomes easy to justify sexual assault when a woman's job is to submit to her husband's every desire. It becomes understandable that queer folks are marginalized and abused when they are understood as threats and less than fully human.

This is the system beneath the surface of modern western Christianity that has been perpetuating a destructive understanding of sexuality and gender for decades and that is now being

17. I must be honest that I hesitated to engage the weighty topic of sexual abuse in this work because I do not have the amount of space necessary to adequately discuss all of the important dynamics of the experience of survivors of abuse and the ways in which Christian theology has been culpable and complicit in it. But after a conversation with a colleague and in order to present a fuller picture of just how destructive patriarchy was towards Jesus, and how destructive it remains in the modern church, I felt convicted that I must at least offer a glimpse into the way sexual assault manifested at Jesus' crucifixion and what that means for the current moment in modern history, where sexual abuse is being exposed more rapidly than ever before. For a deeper dive into this topic, I highly recommend the work of David Tombs and Michael Trainor.

18. #ChurchToo was developed by Emily Joy Allison and Hannah Paasch. Check out their work on Twitter.

revealed for its wickedness through the bravery of women and queer people who are speaking up and making known the evil that has been done to them in the name of so-called "biblical sexuality" or "biblical manhood."

When we begin to understand how the empire used its power of terror to symbolically strip Jesus of his dignity, we will begin to see how the image of the cross can become the subversive key to the liberation of women, queer people, and the socially disadvantaged. When we gaze at the image of Christ crucified, we should be reminded of the grand injustices that are perpetuated by corrupt powers such as patriarchy and motivated to follow in Jesus' subversive path, which seeks to expose and overturn every such system. When we look at the cross, we should likewise become keenly aware of the sexual abuse that Jesus himself was subjected to during his trial, as David Tombs notes:

> The idea that Jesus himself experienced sexual abuse may seem strange or shocking at first, but crucifixion was a "supreme punishment" and the stripping and exposure of victims was not an accidental or incidental element. It was a deliberate action that the Romans used to humiliate and degrade those they wished to punish. It meant that the crucifixion was more than just physical, it was also a devastating emotional and psychological punishment.[19]

Jesus himself faced sexual humiliation and assault at the hands of patriarchy. In this way, God in Jesus stands in radical solidarity with all those who have been victims of sexual violence and trauma and exposes just how damnable such behavior is. Yet, in our modern era, instead of seeing the cross as a glaring reminder of the evil of patriarchy and the way in which Jesus himself faced sexual violence, the church has often used it to justify our own reprehensible manifestations of patriarchy, including the horrific injustice of sexual assault.

19. Tombs, "#HimToo—Why Jesus Should Be Recognised as a Victim of Sexual Violence."

Unless we are willing and able take off our blinders and to see the historical ways in which Jesus on the cross reveals just how damnable the patriarchal ordering of society is and heed the call of our crucified Savior to go into the world embodying the good news of God's liberating dream for the world, we will continue to revert to the destructive heresy of patriarchy. And when we turn away from gazing upon the abused Christ and cling, rather, to the imperial image of a dominator king, we inevitably will begin to allow the reinstitution of the very unjust systems that murdered Jesus and enable sexual abuse in the church today.

Whenever patriarchy is embraced as the primary framework of social ordering, abuse and oppression flourish. Unless we heed the example of Christ to fight the systems of abuse and unjust power, both in the church and outside of it, with every ounce of life within us, we are failing to faithfully follow in the path that Jesus laid out for us to walk upon and enabling patriarchy to destroy the lives of the most vulnerable and marginalized in our communities and beyond. If we are going to take the gospel seriously and align ourselves with the movement of the Spirit towards greater liberation, then we must fight sexual abuse by working to deconstruct the system that enables it to be justified.

Destroying Systems of Domination

From the beginning of Scripture to the final pages of the Book of Revelation, there is a gradual but consistent attack on systems of oppression, dominance, and exclusion. In the incarnation of Jesus, whom Scripture proclaims to be the very revelation of God, we see a radical revolutionary who is willing to lay down his own life in order to show humanity the horror of our dominating, exclusionary behavior and reveal to us a better way. We see a Christ who stands ready to call out and destroy the systems—the "powers and principalities"[20]—that lead to exclusion and oppression, but never

20. Ephesians 6:12.

justified violence or "wrestl[ing] against flesh and blood."[21] Jesus and the apostles understood that the problem wasn't necessarily *bad people*, for individuals had been conditioned to believe that the patriarchal ordering was the way the world should work, but rather *evil systems of power* that find the incarnation and expression through human institutions.

By fighting patriarchy, exposing it as a flawed and deficient way to order our lives and the world around us, we open the possibility of bringing liberation to both the oppressed and the oppressor. Jesus reaches out to and embraces even those who were considered the worst sinners in his day, transgressing cultural and religious boundaries in order to demonstrate that no one stands outside God's redemptive embrace. At the same time, the Jesus of the Gospel accounts is not afraid to speak harsh words to and about the way power is used. And even in the Book of Revelation, Jesus launches a metaphorical battle[22] against the "Satan" (which, by the way, should not be understood as a literal being but the personification of "the accuser,"[23] or the one who makes humanity feel shame) and his army of demonic forces, overcoming them not with brute force but with the power of righteousness.

The image in the Book of Revelation of the Lamb who was slain[24] is a powerful symbol of Jesus' path of liberation. The Lamb is covered in blood, but *not* in the blood of his enemies, rather, his *own* blood, shamefully shed on the cross.[25] This image is the ultimate symbol of the demolishing of all systems of domination such as patriarchy, which is the driving force of *all* oppression in our world today.

The image of the cross, which has been misused for centuries as a symbol to oppress, murder, and discriminate against minorities in every culture is *the* subversive key to our liberation and salvation.

21. Ephesians 6:12.
22. Revelation 12:7–17.
23. Revelation 12:10.
24. Revelation 5:6.
25. Revelation 19:13.

The Just World That God Is Creating

Jesus Christ, in his own body, becomes the *literal incarnation* of liberation from patriarchy. By walking that long and shameful road to Calvary, being publicly mocked and physically murdered, Jesus revealed the fundamental evil embedded in all dominator hierarchies.

Before he is crucified, Jesus event stands before Pontius Pilate and pulls back the veil of the patriarchy, showing that this entire judicial process was nothing more than a spectacle, not intended on dealing justly but on making a show of patriarchal power. Standing before Pilate during his trial, Jesus declares: "I spoke openly to the world . . . I always taught in the temple or in synagogues, where all of the people come together. I had nothing to hide!"[26] He turned the spectacle they were making of him on its head—he proved that he had no desire to overturn their systems of power in order to set himself up as a new earthly emperor, but rather, to reveal "the kingdom of God," which for Jesus meant the world as God always intended it to be. A world where "the wolf will dwell with the lamb, the leopard will lie down with the kid, the calf and the young lion and the fatling will lie together, and a little boy will lead them."[27]

In other words, a world where all of the hierarchies of dominance, *even in the food chain itself,* will be leveled and all creatures will dwell in perfect harmony. This has always been the hope at the heart of the Jewish religion and is at the heart of what Jesus sought to create through his life and teachings. Not a new empire where he and his people rule and reign over everyone else, but a place where *everyone reigns*[28] and *everyone* is declared to be part of the *holy nation and a royal priesthood.*[29]

This is what salvation looks like. *This* is what liberation looks like. It is because of the subversive power of *this* vision that Jesus was crucified. Those who live at the top of social hierarchies are

26. John 18:20, authors paraphrase.

27. Isaiah 11:66.

28. Revelation 20:4–6.

29. 1 Peter 2:9.

easily blinded by privilege and power making it almost impossible for them to see how *equality* could ever be of benefit to them—they believe they are just fine living at the top of the dominator hierarchy. The chief priests and representatives of the empire couldn't believe that Jesus didn't actually want to be "the King of the Jews," but instead desired to work for a world where everyone was equal, where everyone's needs were met, and where everyone was free to reflect the diversity of God in their own unique lives. But Jesus knew that dominance and oppressive power could never bring fulfillment or redemption to the world—only inclusion, equality, self-sacrifice, and love could liberate. And he believed this so deeply that he was willing to walk the road of suffering all the way to the cross.

I believe that if we gaze at the cross long enough, seeking to understand all of the mechanisms that are working at the historic point of crucifixion, we will begin to realize the true power of the gospel of Jesus and recognize that our key to ultimate liberation and salvation as humanity is truly found in the person and work of Jesus.

True Discipleship: Taking Up Our Own Cross

The call for all who call themselves Christians is likewise a call to take up our *own* cross. To participate in the deconstruction of oppressive systems and liberation of the oppressed in our world. It is to follow the kenotic[30] way of Jesus, who "being in the form of God, did not consider equality with God something to be exploited, but he made himself nothing, taking the form of a slave and humbling himself to the point of death, even death on a cross."

This is the path that the church is called to, and all Christians must regularly ask ourselves: How are each of us helping to dismantle these systems of oppression? Are we hiding in our own

---

30. The word kenotic comes from the Greek word kenosis, used by Paul in Philippians 2 to describe the *self-emptying* of Jesus, giving up his position of power and privilege in order to take on human flesh and redeem humanity through sacrificial incarnation.

closets of fear, unwilling to publicly speak up for fear of repercussions? We must know that our silence is being complicit in oppression. Silence is opposed to the gospel. We must, in Christ name, speak up. We must be willing to sacrifice our positions of privilege, power, and comfort in order to lift up the oppressed and give the voiceless back their voices. For the trajectory of biblical revelation, as demonstrated by Jesus, is not a loosening or abolishing of ethical standards, but an expanding of ethical standards to focus not so much on the ritual and religious acts that make one seem pious, but actions that make one a truly ethical person—the sacrificially embodied love for neighbor and self.

Earlier biblical texts emerge from a culture that was in *some* ways not all that different from ours, a culture that desired to keep the oppressed in their oppression in order to uphold the patriarchal system that would keep those with power in power. The revelation of Jesus fundamentally challenges this, which is ultimately why Jesus was crucified—because his ethical revolution posed a serious threat to the oppressive ordering of society in his day, as it does in ours.

If modern Christians are willing to see a clear trajectory of revelation away from slavery and subjugation of women in Scripture, then to be faithful and consistent with scholarship and our hermeneutic approach we also most see the movement of God's Spirit away from the oppression of sexual and gender minorities: these categories cannot and must not be separated. The gospel of Jesus is a gospel of liberation for all oppressed peoples, and unless all of us are liberated together from the grip of patriarchy and every other dominator hierarchy, none of us can ever be truly liberated. Patriarchy is what crucified Christ, and its destruction and the creation of a just and equal world is *the* ultimate hope of the resurrection.

6

Creating Change
The Role of Theology and
the Power of Relationship

Despite there being a clear theological case for LGBT+ inclusion within the Christian tradition, my own experience has taught me that theological debate is not the foundation for changing hearts and minds on this topic. I have spent countless hours debating non-affirming scholars on what Scripture teaches about sexuality and at the end of the day, the argument only seems to solidify each party's position on their opposite sides of the spectrum. While theology is clearly important, what is more important in the Christian tradition is the power of incarnated relationships. The whole of the gospel is the story of a God who took on flesh to be in proximity and in relationship to human beings, and it is through that relational encounter that transformation occurs.

As we already saw, experience has always been an elevated source of authority for Christians, despite the modern fundamentalist position that our experience cannot be trusted. For Peter in Acts 10, it was his *experience* that ultimately changed his mind on the topic of gentile inclusion in the church. When he is called back to the apostolic council in Jerusalem to answer for his unorthodox behavior, he makes two claims: first, he had a personal vision from God that declared gentiles were "clean," and then, he experienced the Spirit falling in an undeniable way on the gentiles as he preached. Both arguments are rooted in personal experience and proximity to those Peter thought of as "other." When the apostles heard Peter's testimony, they did not hesitate to change their theology and celebrate the expansion of God's radically inclusive kingdom.

If the apostles valued experience and allowed it to shape their theology in such a major way then why shouldn't we? If Jesus himself spent time in proximity to those that the religious establishment had deemed outsiders and welcomed them into God's loving embrace, shouldn't we be following that example? No matter which "side" of the theological debate on LGBT+ inclusion you stand on, the biblical imperative is clear: we are called to be in relationship with one another, and only in relationship will God's transforming work manifest powerfully.

For a number of years, I have worked with Auburn Seminary in New York on a research project called *Being in Relationship* which explored how minds were changed around the topic of LGBT+ inclusion specifically among evangelicals and African-American Christian traditions. The research showed that when both parties—LGBT+ and non-affirming—come to the table with a true desire to listen and to empathically learn from one another (as opposed to debating and pre-judging), surrendering the desire to change other minds, meaningful change actually began to occur. Instead of simply telling other stories, living in relationship gave both parties the chance to create and share their stories in real time, and that power of personal witness is what ultimately began the process of transformation.[1]

As part of our research, I have had the opportunity to convene private tables of non-affirming Christians and LGBT+ Christians who come together to simply get to know each other as human beings, and at every meeting the results are always remarkable. Beyond our theological disagreements and different experiences of

---

1. To view the full study, see Auburn Seminary, *Being in Relationship.*

the world, one of the reasons a divide exists so profoundly between LGBT+ Christians and the non-affirming church is simply because *we do not know each other*. What we do know, more often than not, is caricatures of the "other," and we allow that lens to impact the way that we interact with one another. Most non-affirming Christians think LGBT+ Christians are just radical activists who care more about fulfilling their sexual desires than they do conforming their lives to the way of Jesus. Many LGBT+ Christians see non-affirming Christians as uneducated, narrow-minded bigots who only desire to tow the party line to preserve their own power rather than lean into the sacrificial call of Christ to love LGBT+ people. It is only when we come together at these tables and take time to share our stories, dispel the myths, and get vulnerable with one another that true transformation can occur. Non-affirming Christians are forced to wrestle with the profound pain that they have been culpable in causing and the overwhelming reality of the Holy Spirit's presence working in and through the lives of LGBT+ people. And LGBT+ Christians also are transformed as we see that the very principle Jesus embodied most clearly is actually *true*— when we choose to love our neighbors and even our enemies, they are transformed for good.

In the midst of this reality, it is important that we understand that this particular work is not for everyone, and LGBT+ people shouldn't actively seek to sit at tables with those who have traumatically hurt them until inner-healing has occurred and unless there is a system of support around to ensure their wellbeing. To enter into these types of relationships takes a great deal of healing and bravery, and doing so is only one of a multitude of ways to be an effective change-agent in the church and in the world. On the other hand, in my experience, I have witnessed no more effective way to create meaningful and lasting change than through sacrificial proximity to our "others" and attempting to be in relationship with those who see the world differently.

Now, many will push back and say that right belief should be more important than the power of empathy and experience. Obviously, I believe there is merit to theological discourse and that our theology really does matter. But clinging to disembodied theological statements divorced from incarnated experience is not a Christian way to engage theologically. The entire thrust of the Christian story is that the Divine Logos, the Truth, put on flesh and made his dwelling among us.[2] Any attempt to divorce truth from lived reality is thus an unfaithful way to do Christian theology.

Theologian Alister McGrath says that experience is "an accumulated body of knowledge, arising through first-hand encounter with life."[3] If we're honest, most of what we believe and how we view the world comes from what we've experienced and what we've learned as we've lived. It's easy for traditionalists to articulate all of theological reasons derived from their hermeneutical approach to the Bible why they believe it's not possible to be gay and Christian. But when they gain new knowledge through relationships with LGBT+ Christian that demonstrates that the Spirit of God is powerfully working and moving in the very people their theology has deemed reprobate, they should be drawn back to the Scriptures to look once again at what they believe and how they may have misunderstood. Because when reality and theology clash, it's most often your theology that is the problem.

If we're seeking to be faithful to God in our approach to the topic of LGBT+ inclusion, we *must* be in relationship with those who see things differently. We must be willing to sit at the table together and form deep, meaningful relationships across the ideological divide. And in the midst of the relationships that emerge, we also must keep our hearts open to hearing a fresh word from the Holy Spirit which may call us to a different perspective or posture on this topic. If our desire is Christian faithfulness and not simply staking our flag in the ground and defending our theological camp, then we should be eager to listen and learn with humility from those who see things differently. And as we do, I am convinced that the Spirit of God will begin to draw us near to the best way of living, loving, and believing in regard to LGBT+ inclusion in the church—radical inclusion.

2. John 1:14.

3. McGrath, Christian Theology: An Introduction, 192–95.

7

A Faith Worth Believing
Applying the Gospel of Inclusion

When we begin to understand that the entire trajectory of Scripture points to God's radically inclusive love for all of creation, we will be compelled to rethink our entire theological framework. Since patriarchy and exclusion are embedded in the worldview of the writers of Scripture, we will be brought into conflict with various exclusive texts and the doctrines that have formed around them. But this is perhaps the most faithful posture to engage Scripture with—it is the posture of Jesus as he seeks to amend and raise the ethical standards of the Hebrew Bible time and time again in the Gospel accounts; it's the way that the ancient Jewish rabbis engaged Scripture as they wrote out the Talmud, and it's the way that Peter and the early apostles engaged their long-held beliefs—asking hard questions, observing the work of the Spirit around them in their contemporary context, and shifting their beliefs and perspectives to align with reality and the direction that the Spirit seemed to be nudging them. The call away from an exclusive understanding of the Bible invites us to rethink how we view God, how we understand salvation, and how we interact in the world as disciples of Christ.

One of the primary ways that leaning into an inclusive understanding of Christianity leads to spiritual reformation in an individual's life is by calling us out of a dualistic way of interacting in the world, towards what my mentor and renowned philosopher Ken Wilber calls an "integral" approach to the world. In Acts 10, when God speaks to Peter, telling him to stop thinking through the lens of "clean" and "unclean," he's actually being called out of a dualistic binary towards an integral way of viewing the world. Instead of seeing one group, kind, or class of people as the "in" group and another as the "out," the voice in Peter's vision reveals God's true heart: all things can and will be declared "clean." There is no longer a separation between the Jewish people and the gentiles, but in Christ all are integrated into *one new humanity.*

God's plan of redemption is deeply and radically inclusive: God seeks to bring everyone into redemption and reconciliation, leaving no one out. If this is how we begin to understand God— the inclusive Creator of all, who seeks to redeem all—then every aspect of our faith is transformed. We no longer cling to theological purity or doctrinal certainty as a means of knowing that we're truly "saved"—instead, we see that God's plan has always been to "save" everyone, in the midst of all of our diversity. We no longer view the world as those who are children of God and those who are not—for we know that God's heart is for all to be reconciled to their Father. We no longer look at the world as black and white, but as a beautiful rainbow of color, where absolutely everyone has a place. When our faith moves outside of a dualistic system and into the contours, textures, and tensions that exist in reality, it becomes a more versatile, credible, and sustainable faith to build our lives around.

Another way that embracing the gospel of radical inclusion fundamentally transforms us is in our own life and relationships. In my book *True Inclusion,* I spend a hundred pages exploring the implications of the gospel of inclusion on our faith, so I won't reiterate all of those ways here; however, when we understand that the plan that the Spirit of God has been unravelling throughout the ages is to include and redeem absolutely everyone, then we are forced to confront and challenge our own prejudice and bias.

It is a sad reality that throughout its history the church of Jesus Christ has been an often exclusive and damaging body of people. Our failure to see what God has been up to throughout Scripture has led us to reinforce binary way of engaging the world, creating communities that exclude and marginalize the very people God delights in. The church, at various times and places, has discriminated en masse against people of certain races, genders, cultures, theologies, political positions, disabilities, sexualities, and just about every other aspect of identity, and done so in the name and under the authority of Jesus Christ. In our individual lives, many of us have digested this exclusive faith and incarnated it into our existence—distancing ourselves from people who are different from us.

But if we are to learn anything from the example of the life of Jesus, we should take away the fact that true growth and transformation comes from being in proximity with our "others." It is easy to demonize and exclude from a distance, but it's incredibly difficult to continue to marginalize people that we enter into relationship with. It's easy to fail to see how God may be working through those who look and live different to us when we only know them by their social media profile or caricature. But when you're walking through life in close proximity to those who are different, you will often see God moving and speaking in the most unexpected places.

If we take the imperative of the gospel seriously—to "go into the world proclaiming the good news"—then we must be willing to move out of our comfort zones in our own lives and purposely seek out relationships with those who are profoundly different to us. We must confront the dualism and prejudices in our own hearts that we have justified with our exclusionary theology, and seek to follow in the example of Jesus who, as Eugene Peterson wrote, "became flesh and blood and moved into the neighborhood."[1] Fr.

---

1. John 1:14, The Message.

Richard Rohr expands upon the inclusive incarnationality of Jesus, saying:

> The point of the Christian life is not to distinguish one-self from the ungodly, but to stand in radical solidarity with everyone and everything else. This is the full, final, and intended effect of the Incarnation.[2]

Are you willing to move into the neighborhood with those who may even perceive you as an enemy? Are you up to the challenge of overcoming your misconceptions and biases against others? Are you willing to do the hard work to see the light of Christ in "everyone and everything"? The process isn't easy, and if Jesus life teaches us anything it's that such a posture may even come with great pain and our own exclusion, but if we're going to claim to follow Jesus, it seems to me that we have no other choice but to be such radical ambassadors of reconciliation in our world.

Embracing the gospel of inclusion *is* what it means to follow Jesus Christ. In my understanding, there is simply *no other way* to be faithful to the life and teachings of Jesus if we aren't willing to cross all of the culturally defined boundaries and borders that separate us and seek to see that the same Spirit that is within us is actually in and through *everybody else*. In this sense, we're *not* special. God does not play favorites, and therefore, neither should we. Each of us, in all of our diversity and disagreement, is invited to step into our identity as children of God and to work to heal the world through the good news of reconciliation and redemption in Christ. This is and has always been the heart of the Christian faith, though it has often been buried underneath the false gospel of exclusivity, and until we're ready and willing to deconstruct our own faith and, indeed, our own lives and rebuild them around Spirit-driven faith of Christ, we will remain preaching and believing a gospel that is deficient to save our own souls, let alone the entire world. The good news is *great joy for all people*, without exception, inviting us to recreate the world as God has always intended it to be, where all people, in all of our difference, stand united as a multicolored glass mosaic through

2. Rohr, *The Universal Christ*, 33.

which the Light of God shines, bringing beauty and hope to our lives and to our world. I don't know about you, but for me, that sounds like a faith worth believing.

Conclusion
Let the Revolution Begin

In the Book of Acts, chapter 5, there is a profound moment when the apostles are about to be thrown into prison for proclaiming the gospel in Jerusalem and one of the Jewish religious leaders, a man named Gamaliel, speaks up on behalf of the apostles. Gamaliel put's his neck on the line for a group of people whom he clearly didn't agree with, but whom he recognized that God was using in a unique way. Speaking to the entire Sanhedrin, the Jewish ruling body, he declares these powerful words:

> Men of Israel, consider carefully what you intend to do to these men. Some time ago Theudas appeared, claiming to be somebody, and about four hundred men rallied to him. He was killed, all his followers were dispersed, and it all came to nothing. After him, Judas the Galilean appeared in the days of the census and led a band of people in revolt. He too was killed, and all his followers were scattered. Therefore, in the present case I advise you: Leave these men alone! Let them go! For if their purpose or activity is of human origin, it will fail. But if it is from God, you will not be able to stop these men; you will only find yourselves fighting against God.[1]

This passage of Scripture has always stood out to me because of the common sense of it. Gamaliel doesn't believe in Jesus and doesn't support the apostles. However, he clearly is at least open to the

---

1. Acts 5:35–39.

reality that God sometimes works outside of the parameters of his own faith and understanding, and after witnessing the Spirit move through the apostles, he was willing to speak up on their behalf before the Jewish authorities and essentially say:

> If these men are actually heretics and apostates, they will fail like all of the other would-be Messiah's and their failed revolutions. But if these men are doing the work of God, by opposing them we will only find ourselves fighting against God himself.

This argument seems incredibly apt when talking about inclusion, especially of the LGBT+ community. The non-affirming church has spent so much time and energy fighting off the threat of LGBT+ Christians, who are seeking to be a part of the church and to give their lives to following Christ, and despite their best efforts to keep us out, they have failed. Thousands of LGBT+ people are rediscovering Jesus as the key to their spiritual liberation and are stepping into their rightful place at the table of grace. I have had the great honor of traveling all around the world visiting with LGBT+ Christian communities that are emerging in every corner of the globe with zeal and passion for proclaiming and embodying the radical gospel of inclusion, despite the non-affirming church's best efforts to keep them at bay.

I think of my friend, Dr. Aaron Bianco, a Catholic theologian and the former pastoral associate at St. John the Evangelist Church in San Diego, CA. Dr. Bianco is as faithful a follower of Christ as anyone you will ever meet, a man dedicated to living and loving like Jesus. While serving as an openly gay, married pastoral associate in San Diego, radical right-wing, non-affirming Christians began to publicly lambast him, posting photos of his family and his home on the internet, encouraging people to show up and protest his leadership role in the Catholic Church. He faced physical assault after a mass he attended and his church was broken into with the words "No Fags" painted on the wall of a conference room. Dr. Bianco fought hard to resist giving into cynicism or fear, because he knows that God has invited him to lead in the church, but eventually, he was forced to resign from his position for the safety of his family and his parish. However, Dr. Bianco hasn't given up. He continues to speak, teach, and raise his voice on behalf of the millions of LGBT+ Catholics around the world who desire to express their faith and live authentic lives as LGBT+ individuals created in the image and likeness of God. Dr. Bianco has suffered horrendous persecution for simply *desiring to be Christian*. And yet despite the non-affirming church's best efforts, his faith remains steadfast and the Spirit of God continues to provide new opportunities and platforms for Dr. Bianco to share his story and proclaim God's good news to everyone who will listen.

I think of another dear friend, a member of my church, Rev. Gary Matson, who was a prominent Baptist pastor in Colorado, until he was exiled by his own best friend and removed from his church simply because he was gay. Gary struggled for years to find healing from his sexuality so that he could live out his calling to pastoral ministry, participating in reparative therapy programs and marrying a woman as a means of trying to be "faithful" to what "God desired." Despite all of the failed attempts to change and the vitriol of his friends and colleagues in ministry, Rev. Gary continues to serve as a pastor, mentor, and friend to countless LGBT+ Christians at our church, Missiongathering, and beyond. His commitment to following Jesus and living into his calling to be a minister of the gospel remains unshakable, despite the non-affirming church's best attempt to declare him disqualified.

It is the strangest thing, isn't it, that the church, which believes that the mission of God is to bring salvation to the world, continues to fight so hard to keep eager, willing individuals outside of the fellowship of faith? Could anyone truly imagine any of the apostles or Jesus himself declaring someone *unworthy* of following him? To exclude them from serving him? And yet, a majority of the church of Jesus Christ continues to fight with remarkable zeal to declare LGBT+ Christians *unworthy* of following Jesus and serving in the church simply because we disagree on sexual ethics.

The church would do well to heed the warning of Gamaliel in the Book of Acts, and stop opposing the movement of God in and through LGBT+ people. If our movement is of human origins, it will fail. But if it is from God, then it is safe to say that a majority of the church of Jesus Christ is working extremely hard to oppose God himself, and they will fail.

From where I stand, there is simply no question that any movement of people desiring to follow Jesus and be a part of the fellowship of faith is of God. There is no doubt that the hundreds of thousands of LGBT+ Christians around the world that gather in places like Q Christian Fellowship Conference, the European Symposium of LGBT+ Christians, and The Reformation Project are evidence of the ongoing work of God to make manifest the kingdom on earth as it is in heaven. As LGBT+ people, along with other groups that have been marginalized throughout Christian history, continue to step into our rightful place in the church, everything will continue to be transformed. Our theology, which has centered and privileged European, heterosexual, cisgender men, will be completely deconstructed, allowing the radically subversive gospel of Jesus to emerge once again in its place. This mighty movement of the Spirit of God cannot and will not be stopped, an unless the non-affirming church is willing to humble itself and repent of its blindness, it seems likely that it will continue to lose relevance and influence in the world—and thanks be to God for that.

We are living in an era of human history where absolutely *everything* is being transformed. We stand on the brink of an unprecedented moment where those who have been made voiceless for thousands of years are regaining their voice and using it to speak truth to power and dismantle every system of oppression at work in the church and in society as a whole. Just look around—millions of people are gathering in the streets of major cities around the world to march for gender equality, racial justice, and economic justice. More women, people of color, and LGBT+ people were elected to office during the 2018 Midterm Elections in America than ever before in the history of the United States. Countries that enforce homophobic public policies are being pressured by the international community to change or face severe consequences. There are women, people of color, and LGBT+ people now serving in the highest levels of leadership in nearly every Christian denomination in the world, including the Episcopal Church, the United Methodist Church, the Disciples of Christ, the United Church of Christ, the American Baptist Church, the Church of England, the Church of Ireland, the Church of Scotland, and even the Roman Catholic Church. The world is changing, and for those who have eyes to see, it really does seem like what Rev. Dr. Martin Luther King Jr. said is true: "The arc of the universe is long and it bends towardss justice."[2] In the midst of the plethora of crises we face as a species, there is a ray of light, a glimmer of hope, as the oppressive structures that have given birth to most of our crises are finally being dismantled and a radically inclusive society is being birthed in its place.

God is up to something. A reformation, a revolution, a revival is taking place in every corner of the world. As is often the case, those who are righteous in their own eyes[3] are the ones who are blind to the movement of God right in front of them. But for those who have eyes to see and ears to hear, it seems that the church's best days are ahead of it, a day when we once again begin to reflect the inclusive vision of Jesus for the world.

This is what the gospel of Jesus Christ has always been about—the redemption of absolutely everyone through inclusion into the kingdom God. May the powerful wind of the Spirit of God blow away that which blinds us and give us fresh eyes to see with the eyes of our Creator, who declares each person to be a beloved child and who stands, arms outstretched, waiting to welcome each and every one of us home.

2 Craig, "Wesleyan Baccalaureate Is Delivered by Dr. King," 4.

3. Proverbs 21:2.

Appendix 1
Answering Common Questions and Objections

Is the topic of sexuality and gender identity a matter of Christian orthodoxy?

If by orthodoxy we mean the set of doctrines that define the core of historic Christian belief, then *no*, sexuality and gender are not a matter of Christian orthodoxy. There is *no mention* in the creeds of sexual ethics, nor was sexuality or gender identity ever debated in the councils as a matter of determining someone's faithfulness. Frankly, if we're going to move beyond traditional orthodoxy and talk about biblical orthodoxy, the only "belief" that someone must express in order to be "saved," according to Romans 10:9 is the belief that "Jesus is Lord" and that God raised him from death, and I know many people with various sexualities and gender identities that profess these fundamental Christian beliefs every day of their lives. For anyone to declare to someone cannot believe in an affirming theological paradigm and be an "orthodox" Christian is absolutely ridiculous and cannot be justified by any standard from church history or Scripture. Besides, we are saved by *faith alone*, through *grace alone*, in *Christ alone*—not based on our right or wrong beliefs.

I believe this is the first true step towards progress—when the non-affirming church can finally admit that LGBT+ Christians are *in fact* real, authentic Christians and our orthodoxy and salvation do not rise and fall on our theology of sexuality, sexual ethics, or gender, then perhaps the church will become the community of grace that God desires it to be, and perhaps we can taste of the unity that Christ prayed would be our reality on earth as it is in heaven.

Can God change my sexuality or gender identity? Should I pursue change?

This question gets really tricky really quickly. First, any question that begins with "Can God . . ." is usually not a very helpful question because of course the answer is "yes." If God is the eternal Creator and Sustainer of all that is, it is obvious that God *can* do anything. The more important question is *will* God change your sexuality or gender identity? Should you seek out "healing" or "change"? To that, my answer is straightforward and simple: No. Throughout college, I participated in a program to heal my queer sexuality—every week we would work through traumatic events from my childhood and then ask God to bring healing to each one of those areas in hope that by healing my past trauma, I would heal my sexual orientation. (This theory is one of the bedrocks of "conversion therapy.") As we worked through my traumas and invited God to bring healing, I did, in fact, experience transformation. I became desensitized to some of my deep wounds and I was able to find true healing and reconciliation with parts of my story. But after an entire year of this "healing" work, my sexuality hadn't shifted an inch. In fact, the more whole and healthy I felt, the surer I was of my sexual identity.

My story is clearly not everyone's story—there are those who really claim to have been healed of their same-sex attractions or gender dysphoria, and I would never seek to invalidate someone's personal story or experience. Because I believe that sexuality and gender are fundamentally fluid for many people, I absolutely believe that people may experience different attractions or identities at different intensities throughout their lives. But being able to begin dating or having a sexual relationship with the opposite sex does not mean you've been healed—it simply shows the fluidity of sexuality and gender.

Because I believe that queer sexualities and gender identities are part of God's beautiful creation and reflect God's glory, my theology doesn't have room for the belief that God *desires* to change anyone's sexuality or gender. Rather, God wants to call us deeper into our unique identity, because it is in our uniqueness and diversity that we best reflect God's divinity. LGBT+ people have no reason to seek to change their identities or any component of themselves—they are beautiful reflections of God's creativity just as they are. The hard journey is to *accept* that as truth and know it deep in your bones, despite what culture, society, or the non-affirming church might say.

So, to be clear, I think conversion therapy and attempts to change sexuality or gender identity are generally harmful, psychologically irresponsible, and spiritually abusive. I can see no biblical reason for an LGBT+ person to seek to change who God made them to be, and would instead encourage the non-affirming church to listen for how God may be trying to change *its* posture towards and understanding of LGBT+ inclusion.

The Christian tradition has maintained that homosexual relationships are sinful for two thousand years. Why should we think we are wiser than this tradition?

This is perhaps one of the most legitimate questions asked by non-affirming Christians—especially those of Anglican, Catholic, and Orthodox backgrounds, who all see tradition as authoritative. The argument that the church has been unified for most of its history on the topic of LGBT+ is, in some sense, true. The people who have held the most power and who were given the privilege of defining orthodoxy and ethics for the universal Christian church have, pretty uniformly, condemned homosexuality. But therein lies the problem. While I do believe tradition has a place in our theological discernment, I don't believe for a second that we can justify a belief based on the fact that it's what most people have believed.

For much of church history, to disagree with the official teaching of whatever denomination of Christianity ruled in your country was not a matter of debate and disagreement, but would impact your ability to live life freely in society. If you were to be declared a "heretic," you could be imprisoned or killed. As you can imagine, this is a pretty effective way to create uniformity in any group of people. This doesn't mean that people haven't always been free thinkers and haven't always doubted or rejected "official teachings" since the very beginning, but rather, they kept their doubts quiet in order to preserve their own lives.

If Christianity hadn't been co-opted by the Empire, I firmly believe that there would be *millions more* denominations and versions of Christianity around the world. I also believe the question of homosexuality and gender would have been addressed in a more "mainstream" Christian context hundreds if not thousands of years before it was.

Any student of church history knows that everything that is considered "orthodoxy" today was a product of imperial influence—the early church fathers that were appointed to the Councils at Nicaea, Chalcedon, etc., were people that had risen through the ranks because they proved themselves to be faithful to the Emperor. When those councils formulated the doctrinal statements now known as the "creeds," they were seeking to create uniformity for the sake of unifying one holy Christian empire. The motives, therefore, were not pure. This is precisely why the councils took the charge of heresy so seriously—it wasn't a spiritual threat to lay people, but a tangible threat towards imperial allegiance among the people. In their day as in ours, difference is dangerous, and conformity is king when it comes to maintaining power and privilege.

It's also simply not true to say that the church has always been unified in its ethics regarding sexuality and gender—there have always been divergent views, even among the so-called "orthodox," and our understanding of sexuality and gender has evolved significantly, even in conservative churches today.

Finally, if we believe the underlying premise of this entire book, that the Spirit of God is still speaking, revealing truth progressively over time, we must be willing to challenge and move past traditional understandings in order to see the full picture of what God desires. The church has always been willing to change its perspective when prompted by the Spirit—whether on social issues like women and slavery, or on a plethora of other major theological issues, such as those that were debated during the Protestant Reformation and Vatican 2. Tradition should certainly inform our study of theology and ethics, but it cannot be an anchor which holds us in outdated and archaic beliefs and ethics that cause tangible harm to others and prevent the expansion of God's kingdom. Ultimately, I rest peacefully knowing that since Jesus constantly transgressed the ancient Jewish tradition from whence he came, we're in good company when we question and transgress our own Christian tradition in the direction from exclusion to embrace.

How can we engage the topic of transgender inclusion in the church? It seems entirely different to the discussion of LGB inclusion

I believe that it's absolutely correct to say that the topic of transgender inclusion is wholly different than LGB inclusion because we're speaking about *gender identity* as opposed to *sexual orientation*. Transgender people may fall anywhere along the sexuality spectrum from straight to gay to asexual, just like anyone else. Because transgender identity generally has nothing to do with sexuality, the theological case for transgender inclusion in the church is completely different than that of queer sexuality. I won't pretend for a second to be an expert at explaining the theology for transgender inclusion, and there are many who have done a much better job than I ever could.[1]

1. The best resource on this topic is a book by my friend Austen Hartke, a

However, I actually believe transgender inclusion in the church is a much easier biblical case to make, because it's more self-evident. Christians believe that in the fall of humankind into sin, every aspect of creation was impacted. It is sin that gives birth to all of the hardships that humanity faces. It's quite easy to believe then that there are a good number of people who may be born in a body that is not congruent to their inner identity. Many transgender individuals experience gender dysphoria, a psychological term that refers to the profound distress one can feel when one lives life in a body that presents as something other than their true identity. I don't believe that gender dysphoria is God's desire for anyone, and believe that the transgender person's journey to reconcile their inner-identity with their physical identity is a holy and good process. Unless one is willing to say that *all attempts* to change the body in any way are sinful—including surgery and medicine—then how could we say that a transgender person's journey to align with who God made them to be is anything but a holy process? Again, I am not an expert in transgender theology and at the end of the day, my recommendation is to listen and learn from the growing number of transgender Christian leaders gaining public platforms, like my friends Paula Stone Williams, Allyson Robinson, and Austen Hartke, who articulate their personal experience and their own journey to reconcile their faith and gender identity in powerful ways.

What is a liberated, progressive Christian sexual ethic?

As we begin to rethink our understanding of sexuality and gender as Christians, it is natural to begin rethinking our general ethic of sex and relationships, since these all are fundamentally linked. I know a great deal of LGBT+ Christians and allies who try incredibly hard to maintain a tight grip on "conservative sexual ethics" as they lean into their theology of inclusion, but frankly, I don't

---

transgender theologian, *Transforming*.

believe it's a sustainable or logically consistent path. If we accept that the Holy Spirit is at work to deconstruct the systems that have oppressed humanity for centuries, namely patriarchy, then we must also examine how patriarchy has shaped our understanding of sex and relationships. There are many brilliant theologians and ethicists who have done and are doing this work (including Margret Farley, Patrick Cheng, Marcella Althaus Reid, Nadia Bolz Weber, and Matthias Roberts), but for the sake of brevity, I'll just give you a quick summary of my perspective.

First, most of what the church has condemned throughout history has little to no biblical basis. For instance, if you ask almost any traditional Christian if premarital sex is sinful, they will immediately say "Yes!" But ask them to show you where that comes from in Scripture and they will be forced to admit that there is *not a single verse that says sex is only intended for a marriage relationship.* In fact, all the biblical passages that have been translated as speaking of "fornication"—which does mean sex outside of marriage—have been retranslated in many modern Bible translations because scholars realized that the original Greek word *porneia* actually has no clear definition, but contextually, certainly refers to sexual relations with a prostitute. (The root of *porneia* is a Greek term meaning "arch," which is a reference to physical location that individuals would purchase sexual favors from prostitutes.) Generally, the only clear condemnations of sexual activity in Scripture are either rooted in patriarchy or are behaviors that most people throughout history up to the modern day would condemn—sex with your parents, sex with your siblings, sex with animals, etc. So if we're going to be honest about what the Bible teaches, we have to say that it actually says *very little* about sexual ethics.

With that said, I base my personal sexual ethics on Romans 14, a passage where Paul addresses division in the church around culturally defined ethics—some people think it's good to eat only vegetables and some think its good to eat meat. Some people believe they should celebrate holy days, others see every day as holy. Paul then essentially instructs the church to listen to the voice of their conscience, the voice of God within us, the law of God written on our hearts. If something seems to violate our conscience, Paul says, then it's sin. But if something doesn't violate our conscience, even if someone else thinks it's a sin, we shouldn't fear judgment nor should we pass judgment.

It's a beautiful passage that reflects the raw, reality of ethics and morals—they are always hyper contextual and based on individual circumstances and experiences. I believe there are some core virtues that Scripture outlines—I typically look to the list Paul calls "the fruit of the Spirit"—and ask whether my action reflects these values. If it does, I have good reason to believe it's moral and ethical. If it doesn't, then perhaps it's not. As we all seek to incarnate these values together, they will look different in each of our lives, but the call is to encourage one another to seek to honor these values and refuse to shame or judge those who come to different conclusions than us.

So, when we ask, for instance, if premarital sex is a sin, I would invite us to reflect on whether premarital sex embodies love, joy, peace, patience, kindness, goodness, faithfulness, gentleness, and self-control. If for you it *does* then how could we call it sinful? For some people or in certain circumstances, our impulse to have sex may be greedy, selfish, and a mere pursuit of pleasure as we disregard the value of the other—that kind of sex is clearly *not* ethical or moral; it violates the way God has wired humans to interact.

Many non-affirming Christians will say this is just a slippery slope towards abusive and unhealthy expressions of sex such as pedophilia or bestiality—which, of course, is absurd. There is literally *no way* that sex with a minor or an animal could embody the values at the core of the gospel, and therefore, there is literally no coherent Christian case that could be made to endorse such practices.

So, to summarize, I believe that if we're centered on the values of the New Testament and we seek to live them out faithfully in our own lives (and stop trying to enforce ethical rules in others' lives) it seems likely that we will embody health, wholeness, and holiness in the ways that we engage in sexual activity.

How should Christians think about non-monogamous relationships?

This question is perhaps the most controversial in the modern theological conversation around sexual ethics, but to me seems to be one of the simplest to answer. While it is absolutely true that *most* relationships throughout human history and the Christian tradition traditions have focused on the union of two individuals, it's also true that monogamy is not the only equation for human relationships, both in human society and in the Christian tradition. Throughout the Bible, there are dozens of examples of non-monogamous relationships that are deemed to be acceptable and even blessed. Neither the Hebrew Bible nor the New Testament condemn non-monogamous relationships. In cultures around the world, non-monogamous relationships have been normative for thousands of years and only began to be seen as problematic when European Christian colonizers appeared on their shores and declared them to be so.[2]

At the heart of a Christian relational ethic should be the value of commitment and covenant, and many non-monogamous relationships are centered on a deep and enduring commitment of more than three people to walk in relationship with each other throughout life. Logically and ethically, I can see no reason to deem such relationships to be unethical or sinful.

The angst around this question comes from a deep misunderstanding among Christians about what *polyamory*, the most prominent form of non-monogamy in the Western World, is all about. Most polyamorous people I have met would argue that they have been relationally wired to be able to form deep, committed, loving relationships with more than one other person. The relationships they form may include two or three other people, and all of those individuals are in some way relationally committed to one another. Polyamory, therefore, is not equivalent to promiscuity. If individuals come together in committed relationship, I believe

---

2. For some modern examples of non-monogamy around the world, check out https://matadornetwork.com/life/non-monogamy-around-world/.

they are honoring the biblical paradigm for covenant, regardless of the number of people that may be involved.

Polyamory also isn't polygamy—truly polyamorous people seek to give every person an equal amount of power in the relationship, whereas polygamy gives one man power over many women, reinforcing a damaging manifestation of patriarchy. Again, I will not claim to be an expert here, and I know that *many* Christians, even progressive ones, are not willing to think about this question. But I want to reiterate the entire message of this book and say, if we believe the gospel is radically inclusive, we must seek to make space even for the smallest minority of people, and be willing to be in relationship with and think through our own beliefs and worldview in light of their experience. Get to know polyamorous Christians, like Rev. Rachelle Brown, the interim moderator of the Metropolitan Community Church, and allow God to teach and speak through their stories and their lives. You don't have to agree with anyone—just listen and learn. You may be surprised by what God reveals to you.

How should we respond to "Side-B" Christians?

I have many friends and colleagues who would identify as "Side-B" Christians. This is language used in the Gay Christian community to refer to individuals who generally believe that it's not a sin to "be gay" or to experience same-sex attractions, but that it is sinful to act on those attractions. "Side-A" Christians are affirming Christians who believe it is not sinful to express queer sexuality or gender as faithful followers of Jesus.

Side-B individuals typically advocate for celibacy or enter into mixed-orientation marriages—a marriage where a person who is attracted to the same-sex enters into a marriage with a person of the opposite sex in order to honor their convictions that heterosexuality is the only proper paradigm for a marriage to occur. I honor these individuals' stories and choice to live their lives in this manner, but I absolutely disagree with this theology and believe it is deeply harmful when it's advocated as the most faithful or only

Christian path for LGBT+ people. I believe that some people may be called to celibacy, but it is, in fact, a *calling* and not a requirement for anyone. I believe some mixed-orientation marriages work really well and are fulfilling for the people involved. But to declare that this is what God desires for all LGBT+ people is not biblically faithful, psychologically healthy, or realistic. Scriptures proclaim that humans are generally made for relationship—intimate, sexual relationships—with other human beings. This is a regular part of our God-given design and development throughout life. To say that God has created millions of LGBT+ people with sexual desires and relational drives for intimacy, but prohibits them from expressing these natural aspects of their humanity is cruel and unfaithful.

The true danger of the Side-B narrative is that it has become the primary story that non-affirming churches have embraced and love to tell in order to look "welcoming" but is, in reality, not at all different from the most severe exclusive theologies. It allows people to "be gay," but still tells those people that their sexuality is flawed, broken, and cannot be expressed in their lives. If anyone does express their sexuality and enters into a same-sex relationship, they are deemed sinners and excluded from their rightful place at the table of grace. As my friend Pastor Colby Martin aptly (but admittedly crassly) puts it, this is a "chocolate-covered turd," which makes the theology and approach seem sweet and inviting, but it's still the same "crappy," destructive theology of exclusion underneath.[3]

Despite my strong opinions here, the reality is that Side-B Christians exist and there should be room for them at the table, too. While I will always be quick to call out the dangers of their theological paradigm, I also must seek to ensure that their stories and lives are honored alongside those of everyone else. I firmly believe that there should always be room in our churches and our theology for Side-B Christians, but their position must not be seen as the *normative* or *best* expression of faith and sexuality for a majority of LGBT+ Christians, since I believe it perpetuates the same

3. See Martin, "The Newest Non-LGBTQ-Affirming Approach."

oppressive theology that Christ seeks to liberate us from. The Side-B position is often a necessary step along a person's theological journey, but it should not be seen as the *end* of that journey.

How can I be a good ally to the LGBT+ Christian community?

There is a growing movement of straight allies within Christian communities that are being ignited with passion to advocate on behalf of their LGBT+ siblings in Christ, and for that I am incredibly grateful! But asking the question of how to be an effective and "good" ally is an important one, because often overly-eager allies cross boundaries and do things that may be well intentioned but cause harm to the LGBT+ people they are seeking to help.

One of the biggest mistakes I see allies make over and over again is being ignited with passion for LGBT+ people and immediately seek to build a platform, whether public or just within their community, as "the advocate." This could look like blogging, writing books, organizing speaking events, starting non-profits, leading groups focused on LGBT+ topics, etc. Now, obviously, there is a place for straight allies to have platforms and to speak up about LGBT+ inclusion to audiences that may not be quick to hear LGBT+ people themselves. But *more often than not*, there are LGBT+ people who are ready and able to speak up and act up for our own inclusion who are denied platforms simply because of their queer identity and when multitudes of straight allies continue to step up and build platforms on *our* stories and experiences, they're actually only perpetuating the system of oppression against queer people.

One of the primary roles of ally should not be to be a voice for the voiceless, *but to give the voiceless back their voice*; to use heterosexual or cisgender privilege to get queer people access to spaces and platforms where we can have a seat at the table, where we can share our own experiences, and where we can be seen and heard as legitimate human beings and Christians. Again, this is how research has consistently shown that change happens—not through having straight folks argue theology or even advocate on our behalf, but through *LGBT+ people telling their own stories and declaring their own truth*. Strategically this is the most effective way to create change, and from a justice perspective, I believe it is the *right and just* path.

Another role for those of you who are allies is to seek to do your own research into the queer community, our history, and our culture. Any minority group will usually express frustration about the need to keep "educating" the dominant groups about their experience of reality—it does get exhausting and frustrating to keep explaining, when I identify with the word "queer," why we have pride parades, and the theological rationale for being a gay Christian. What is refreshing and a blessing to me is when I interact with an ally who clearly has *done the work* and knows a great deal about what it means to be an LGBT+ Christian. For instance, a great example of someone who is an incredibly well-informed ally is Kathy Baldock, a straight, cisgender woman who has spent years supporting LGBT+ people and doing her own extensive research.

The final crucial role of allies is to be support systems for the LGBT+ people in your life. Oftentimes, we've experienced a lot of rejection. Oftentimes we are hesitant to reach out when we feel alone or depressed. Allies who step up and offer hospitality, encouragement, and support become profound channels of healing and redemption in the lives of LGBT+ people. Having the support of others and knowing that others will have our backs if we ever do face marginalization or rejection because of who we are is one of the most powerful gifts you can give an LGBT+ person. At the end of the day, I would encourage allies to just *do your best* and *keep showing up* for your LGBT+ siblings. We need you, we love you, and we are grateful for you.

Appendix 2
Selected Writings on Inclusion

I have been writing about the topic of LGBT+ inclusion in the public arena for nearly eight years, from advocating for civil marriage equality to critiquing political leaders for their perpetuation of harmful patriarchal ideals, all aiming to be practical and inspiring to the general layperson who may be reading the piece. It is my hope that some of these writings may be helpful to you, the reader, as you move from thinking about the technical side of this conversation—where we explore cultural context, language, and theology—and move towards practical application of a theology of inclusion in your own life and world.

"God Is on the Move: Evangelical Response to SCOTUS Ruling for Equality."
Huffington Post, June 26, 2015

Just a few hours ago, I was standing on the steps of the Supreme Court as the ruling on marriage equality was announced. The weight of the moment was almost too much to bear. The surge of exuberant joy and peace that flowed through my body caught me by surprise. As we heard the announcer's words echo across the marble platform, I became keenly aware that this was far more than a change in our laws. There was something much bigger occurring in this moment.

As a follower of Jesus, I realized that this ruling for equality is an undeniable result of the Spirit of God moving in our midst, calling his church, our nation, and our world forward towards redemption, reconciliation, and restoration. Throughout the whole of human history, we have seen the Spirit inching humanity closer and closer towards a vision of a renewed world where justice, equality, and beauty reign. Jesus called this new reality the kingdom of God.

As the subtle winds of God's Spirit continue to blow at our backs, causing us to progress closer to a truly just and equal world, I believe we are going to continue to see moments like this one, where oppressed minorities will at last partake in the sweet experience of liberation.

Though many of my evangelical brothers and sisters may disagree, as I have worked among the LGBTQ community and evangelical leaders over the past year, I have become absolutely convinced that all of the change we see occurring is not a result of Christians bowing the knee to cultural trends, but Christians awakening to what God is saying to our world. And God is saying that all people—gay, straight, bisexual, lesbian, queer, transgender, questioning, asexual—were all created in the eternal, expansive, and creative image of God and should be embraced, welcomed, and dignified as such. The ruling we've seen today is a major movement of God's Spirit, but we still have a long way to go.

In the evangelical church, we must continue to work to help teach our people how to rightly divide the word of truth, instructing them on how to correctly interpret the biblical message based on context and a theology of progress. We need to continue to call the thousands of evangelical leaders who have already changed their minds on questions of LGBTQ inclusion to step forward, no matter what the cost, because it is our duty as followers of Jesus Christ to sacrifice our self interest and comfort for the good of the oppressed.

On the civil level, as Americans, it's clear that we also still have a lot of work to do before we can say that our country is truly equal for all LGBTQ individuals. According to GLSEN, in twenty-eight states, LGBTQ people can still be fired from their job based on their sexual orientation alone. In eight states, LGBTQ inclusive curriculums are prohibited in schools. In thirty-two states, schools have little to no protection for LGBTQ students against bullying. So while this ruling for equality is needed and important, there is still a lot of work to be done in our nation to ensure that equality and justice are a reality for LGBTQ individuals.

And as a member of the LGBTQ community, today is an unbelievably joyous occasion. For far too long, LGBTQ people have been marginalized and oppressed by society, government, and religious institutions in this country. Though the LGBTQ movement has been growing in influence and prominence over the last decade, we still have been a people who were denied basic rights as citizens of this country, which has been a fundamental assault on our dignity as humans.

Today's ruling marks a momentous shift in the consciousness of our nation, where, from the highest levels of power in our country, LGBTQ people and our marriages are seen as worthy of equal respect and status as everyone else. This day has taken far too long, but I am incredibly grateful that it has finally arrived.

God is on the move.

"A Witness to Equality"
Speech at Washington National Cathedral
Patheos, July 1, 2015

The following speech was delivered by Brandan Robertson at the National Cathedral in Washington, DC on June 30th, 2015 as part of the Service Honoring the Road to Equality.

This evening, we gather here in this sacred space to give thanks to God for the dawning of a *new day* in our nation. A day that many in this room, if asked just a few years ago, never believed that they would have lived to see.

Tonight, we gather here to celebrate the Supreme Court's ruling that affirms the fundamental dignity and equality of every single child of God, of every diverse sexual orientation and gender identity.

Tonight, we also gather here to remember those whose lives vanished like a vapor, gone too soon before they could see this beautiful day.

Tonight, I stand here before you and with you with a heart brimming with gratitude and appreciation, both to God and to the thousands of people who have struggled and fought with lives dedicated to ensuring that the dream of equality would one day become our reality.

Beloved, tonight, it *is* our reality.

Just ten years ago, a majority of people of faith in this country were preaching a message of exclusion and condemnation of LGBTQ people. A majority of our political leaders and legislators said same-sex relationships violated the sanctity of marriage.

Just ten years ago, a night like tonight would have been unfathomable. And yet, *here we are.* Everything has changed, for good.

My journey towards coming to terms with my queer sexuality and becoming an advocate and activist for equality has been a rather short one.

Just six years ago, you could have found me on a night like this on a street corner in Baltimore, holding up signs that said "REPENT" and preaching against the dangers of the "gay lifestyle."

I, like so many of you, grew up being taught that my sexual orientation was fundamentally flawed and sinful, and that in order to be a faithful Christian or a whole person, I needed to stand firmly against the "gay agenda," which sought to undermine the "biblical values" that our nation was based upon.

I never had the opportunity to even dream of a day where I might be able to legally marry a person of the same sex, much less to think that it would be blessed by my country and by my God.

But over the years, as my own relationship with God grew in depth and maturity, as I studied the Scriptures and got to know so many beautiful LGBTQ individuals, all of the messages that I had been taught about sexuality and equality began to dissolve. They didn't hold water. They didn't match up with reality.

I tried everything I could to hold on to the teachings of my youth. From religious counselors, to versions of reparative therapy, to cutting off relationships with anyone who identified as openly gay.

But the more I isolated myself and tried to "fix" myself, the more I sensed God's Spirit gently nudging me to stop struggling and to embrace the person that *I fundamentally was created to be*. That I am, in the words spoken from the mouth of God in the story of creation, *"very good"* just the way I am, with all of my intricacy.

My six-year journey has taken me from feeling imprisoned and overwhelmed by the way God had made me, to this place, where I feel fully alive and more hopeful than ever.

My journey has brought me to the place where tonight, standing before you, as a committed Christian and an openly queer man, who now lives in a society where, increasingly, I can live free, embracing all that God has made me to be, without fear of judgment or oppression. What an amazing thing that God has done!

Last week's Supreme Court ruling for equality means that no matter who I fall in love with, we will be afforded the same rights and benefits as every heterosexual couple in this nation.

It means that should I want to begin a family with a partner of the same sex, that our family will be recognized and affirmed by our society. That our marriage no longer needs qualifiers. It isn't a gay marriage or lesbian marriage. It is *marriage. Period.*

It means that my children will grow up in a nation where their family is not seen as "less-than" or "dysfunctional," but rather as one of the many beautiful expressions that love can take.

Friday's decision was a much-needed and beautiful step forward, but let us also be mindful that in the midst of our celebration, there is still a lot of work left be done.

For we still live in a nation where in nearly thirty states, LGBTQ people can *still* be fired based on their sexual orientation or gender identity alone. In the same number of states, there is little to no protection for LGBTQ children from bullying in schools.

And beyond issues of sexuality, we still live in a country plagued by racism, as we were so brutally reminded just a few weeks ago with the horrendous events of Charleston, South Carolina or by the historically African American churches that are burning to the ground all around the Southern United States this week.

Indeed, we as a people continue to make huge steps towards justice, but we still have a *long way to go*.

Out of our celebration and thanksgiving tonight, may we rise up with greater resolve to press harder and louder for justice and equality for all people, both in our nation and around the world.

May this victory we have accomplished propel us to work harder for the victory and dignity for all people in the human family.

And finally, I want to make one more observation. I firmly believe that all of this movement towards justice is part of something far bigger than any of us will ever be able to fully fathom. I believe that Friday's ruling is just one more part of a powerful and ongoing movement of God's Spirit, calling humanity forward towards a more just, a more equal, a more diverse, and a more beautiful reality.

I believe that this ruling for equality, this nation-wide shift in the way same-sex relationships are viewed, even the individual shifts taking place in the hearts and minds of millions of people in our nation, is all a part of something Jesus' called *"the kingdom of God."* Or another way of saying it, all of this is all part of humanity maturing and becoming *more* fully human, *more* connected with God, and *more* unified with one another in all of our diversity and elegance.

We as a people are evolving and moving forward. Our world is getting more complex and more mysterious. God is up to something BIG. And this rushing river of progress *cannot* be stopped. It's flame *will not* be extinguished.

What a tremendous privilege it is for all of us to be apart of this tremendous day.

In this spirit, may we continue to march forward, filled with passion and love, moving along with the rhythms of God's Spirit, to make our lives, our communities, our nation, and our world a place where love truly has the ultimate victory.

A new day has dawned, indeed—and *thanks be to God* that we have arrived here to partake in it *together*.

"The Danger of Disembodied Theology"
Nomad Blog on Patheos, January 14, 2016

After spending almost a week together in "prayer," the Primates of the Anglican Communion have released a statement calling for official "discipline" of the Episcopal church in America until it repents for the changes it has made in its doctrinal position on marriage. In a statement released by the Primates on Thursday, they noted:

> Recent developments in The Episcopal church with respect to a change in their Canon on marriage represent a fundamental departure from the faith and teaching held by the majority of our Provinces on the doctrine of marriage.

They continued on, saying:

> The traditional doctrine of the church in view of the teaching of Scripture, upholds marriage as between a man and a woman in faithful, lifelong union. The majority of those gathered reaffirm this teaching.
>
> . . .Given the seriousness of these matters we formally acknowledge this distance by requiring that for a period of three years The Episcopal church no longer represent us on ecumenical and interfaith bodies, should not be appointed or elected to an internal standing committee and that while participating in the internal bodies of the Anglican Communion, they will not take part in decision-making on any issues pertaining to doctrine or polity.[1]

---

1. Quoted in Handley, "Primates Distance Themselves from the US Episcopal church in Official Statement."

Globally, positions on same-sex marriage and LGBTQ+ inclusion in the church are varied. In the United States, a growing majority of Christians are fully supportive of same-sex relationships. This trend is also reflected in the United Kingdom, Australia, and New Zealand. However, the majority of Christians globally are still opposed to same-sex relationships. There are many reasons for this reality, including a lack of education on issues of sexuality and gender identity, a lack of exposure to theological discourse on these issues, and a lack of cultural acceptance of same-sex relationships.

Whenever I see large Christian bodies making statements like the one released from the Primates Gathering, I also wonder just how many LGBTQ+ people these leaders actually know. These statements not only reflect a lack of education and understanding, but they also reveal a great deal of fear rooted in ignorance. While I don't doubt for a second that the Primates gathered actually believe that the Scriptures teach that marriage is exclusively between one man and one woman, I am also aware that these leaders have likely never taken the time to examine the lives of and hear the stories of those of us who identify as LGBTQ+ Christians.

If Christianity is anything, it's incarnational. Our faith is rooted in the story of God becoming a human being and experiencing life among us, as one of us. Christian faith is rooted in the principle of "kenosis," a theological word used by the apostle Paul in his hymn of praise in his Letter of the Philippians, chapter 2, where he describes how Christ refused to exploit his power and instead stepped into solidarity with humanity, becoming Immanuel, *the God who is with us.* In the Christian story, God himself desires to walk in the shoes of humanity, to experience their reality, and allows that to shape him.

Embedded in this story is the idea that experience shapes our perception of reality. No concept is scarier to Christians, influenced by Western, modernistic, post-Enlightenment thought, than to believe that our *lived experience* and our *emotions* could be key components influencing our concept of truth. But this is a fundamental part of what it means to be a follower of Jesus Christ: that we walk with those whom we perceive as "far off," those who we don't understand, those who we perceive as "sinful." And it is in that process of walking alongside of them that God speaks to us most powerfully and our concept of reality is shaped most drastically.

What I am saying is this: I believe that the Anglican Primates who are calling for separation from the Episcopal church because of its position on same-sex relationships are acting out of fear and ignorance because they have never actually sat across a table from and walked alongside any LGBTQ+ disciples of Jesus. It is easy to demonize from a distance. It's easy to declare "heretic" when you've never walked in the shoes or experienced God through the eyes of your "other." These Primates, and in fact, all those who are animatedly opposed to LGBTQ+ Christians, need to follow the biblical imperative and get to know some faithful LGBTQ+ followers of Jesus. They need experience life through our eyes. They need to see just how God-honoring our relationships and our "lifestyle" can be. Because until they do that, they will only be grasping on to disembodied theology, and nothing is more dangerous, destructive, or deadly.

What does all this mean for the future of the Anglican Communion? As much as many of my conservative friends might think this is a major move that threatens to cause a catastrophe in the communion, I don't think that's even remotely true. The Archbishop of Canterbury said last week that if a schism were to happen, it would be a "failure" to act as a communion of Christians, but it wouldn't be a "disaster." Nonetheless, it is my hope that the Primates aggressive actions will not result in a schism, but rather, will open the door for further conversation and dialogue. Schism should be reserved for only the most severe cases of heterodoxy and immorality, and disagreements on same-sex relationships don't even come close to that.

May God grant the leaders of the Anglican Communion the discernment, grace, and boldness to embrace the incarnate way of Christ, refusing to divide over disembodied doctrines, but to walk in the shoes of the very people over whom they are disagreeing. And may they, in doing so, experience the power of God working in and through the lives of sexual and gender minorities and turn from their resistance to the wild, untamable movement of the Holy Spirit.

"Our Love Must Expel Fear:
On the Orlando Shooting"
June 14, 2016

I was standing at a gay bar in London when news flashed across my iPhone that there was a shooting at an LGBT+ nightclub in Orlando. I was standing in the street with hundreds of other LGBT+ people, conversing, laughing, and celebrating life. I saw the news and my initial reaction was to sigh in disbelief, but to presume that this was just another tragic shooting that I've become all too familiar with hearing about in the US. I whispered a brief prayer for those involved, and I put my phone away and continued to enjoy my time with friends.

I continued on with my evening and the news continued to flash across my phone. The death toll went higher. The suspected motive: terrorism. And the club was targeted because it was an LGBT+ nightclub. That night as I laid down, I was overwhelmed with emotion. I have been on a tour across the UK, speaking on LGBT+ liberation and the importance of embracing our full selves. I have spent nearly an entire week with LGBT+ people, sharing life with them, hearing stories of heartache and pain, and being reminded that we're all truly in this together. I was beginning to feel a spark of hope that things in our world were truly changing for the better. That our churches and our societies were truly awakening to the beautiful gift that is queer people, and that our love was drowning out the hatred and fear.

But as I lay in my bed, a moment of doubt rose in my mind. In 2016, how could such an atrocity still happen? How could a young man, so tormented by his fear of queer love, carry out such an act of hatred? Maybe things hadn't changed so much after all.

In the recent days, as I've watched the news from around the world, as I have seen the displays of support for the LGBT+

community in Orlando, and as I have heard the sacred names of those who were lost in that nightclub read over and over again, I have chosen to believe that hope is not lost.

Every one of those people who were lost in that nightclub were there because that club provided a sanctuary for them to be free, to embrace their truest and fullest selves, and to truly let their light and love shine. Their lives had tasted the liberation that was possible for LGBT+ people in that club and that night, a deeply broken, fearful individual decided to violate that liberation; to cut short their lives because he could not fathom the bigness and beauty of their love.

Their names, faces, and stories speak to us now as witnesses of the power of love, each name and face representing a soul that was on the journey of life, of liberation, of discovering and embracing all that they were created to be. Their lives speak to us, calling us each to step forward, to come out, to confront this act of terror with the power of pride, and to let our love shine forth in the world. There are no answers, no justification, and truly no consolation for the families, friends, and communities of those who died that night.

We must continue to remember the names, the faces, and the stories of every life that was lost, and allow their lives to propel us forward. Some of them were out to their friends and family. Some were not. Some were allies, mothers, and friends. All of them bear witness to us now and call to us to embrace love, to fight fiercely against the ideologies that breed fear and hatred, and to show the world that queer love is true love, that it is the very love of God. Their lives call us to no longer tolerate the beliefs and practices that make LGBT+ people second-class citizens in our world, perpetuating the lie that we are somehow disordered.

The only way to fight such acts of terror is with the power of love. And love does not stay silent. Love speaks out. Love does not allow violence to continue, but works tirelessly to call out the roots of terror and demand that they are changed. This is a message for our churches, our governments, our schools, indeed, every aspect of our world. Nothing less than full inclusion, full acceptance, and full embrace of LGBT+ people is acceptable, for nothing less than that will kill this fear and allow our love to be magnified in your midst.

Fear breeds on misunderstanding and ignorance. It grows when not in proximity to the people that it's against. Fear breeds on separation, allowing us to demonize from a distance. But love calls us together, to union. Love calls us to relationship, to the full embrace of those whom we fear the most. And in that embrace, something miraculous happens. The power of union, of togetherness, of proximity with the ones whom we fear the most transforms us. It expels our fear. And it magnifies love. This is the path that leads to life. This is the path that will expel hatred and fear in our world.

May this unthinkable tragedy cause all of us to pause, to think about what we believe, how we live, and what we want our lives to look like. May the lives of each one lost call us to boldness, empower us to step forward, and enable us to say what needs to be said, do what needs to be done, and be who we were created to be. May each of the forty-nine lives that were lost be our inspiration to do the work and to be the change, no matter what the cost. It is the only way to honor their lives, to rid our world of fear, and to allow love to flourish.

Amen.

"Everything Must Change:
On Privilege, Patriarchy, and Donald Trump"
September 1, 2016

We are in a period of American history in which everything about the way our country has functioned since its inception is being dismantled and deconstructed. Since the very founding of our nation, our leaders have been driven, largely unconsciously, by the power of patriarchy. Patriarchy is, at its most rudimentary level, the belief that men are best suited to lead and are the ideal example of what a human should look like. Built into a patriarchal mindset is a singular image of the supreme man that all of society strives to uplift and honor. For those of us in the Western world, this image has been the straight, white, cisgender, hyper-masculinized, wealthy, Christian man. This is the ideal image of humanity, the kind of person that we need to lead our homes, our churches, and our nation, the only kind of person truly capable of leading us down the path of American idealism. Naturally, of course, this class of men is given power and privilege at the expense of those who do not fit this idealized image—women, people of color, sexual minorities, and those who are seen as "effeminate" men. These kinds of people, who make up the majority of the population, are seen at some level as tools meant to help the idealized humans live the life that they desire, regardless of what position that places these "less-than" humans in.

As a direct result of the unconscious systems of patriarchy, we have seen the systemic oppression of each of these groups throughout our history. And though it is true that much progress has been made, the oppression continues. Women do not get paid fair and equal wages, people of color are imprisoned and killed for minor offenses, and LGBT+ people can be fired because of their sexual orientation or gender identity in more than half of the states in our nation. We are not a nation of equality at all, despite what we are indoctrinated to believe from our politicians and school curriculums. We are a nation that idealizes one type of human, provides privilege, benefits, and protections to one class of person before anyone else. If you're a straight, white, cisgender, man, America is your nation. For you, the sky is the limit. But for the rest of us, in varying degrees, the decks are stacked against us.

Think about it. Until the election of President Barack Obama, our nation has been led *only* by the kind of person that I've described above. But with the election of President Obama, we reached of fundamental tipping point that leveled a devastating blow to the patriarchal systems that have fueled America since our inception. For the first time, a non-white person was given the most powerful position in our nation. Immediately, you'll remember, much of the patriarchal establishment lashed out against Obama, questioning everything from his religion to his place of birth—they couldn't handle losing this most important position which enabled their system of privilege to continue. Over the last eight years, we have continued to see a constant chipping away at the power and influence of patriarchy. Systemic racism has been brought to national consciousness and been dealt many devastating blows through the work of #BlackLivesMatter, the LGBT+ rights movement has gained political power and influence, securing marriage equality for all sexual and gender minorities and fighting to end discrimination once and for all, and now, a woman is the Democratic nominee for president. The patriarchy is crumbling. Power is slipping through the fingers of the privileged, and the way our nation has functioned since its founding is forever being reconfigured.

Naturally, these are scary times for the beneficiaries of the patriarchy. For them, still blinded to the systemic oppression that they have benefited from and perpetuated, this just seems like a moral decline, a threat to the most foundational dreams of our founding fathers. And to some extent, they're right. Those who are chipping away at the patriarchal systems that have fueled our nation *are* threatening many of the values of the founding fathers, who, beyond the idealism of their words enshrined in our constitution, desired to perpetuate patriarchy and create a nation where *they* could survive and thrive on the backs of those whom they believed were less-than-ideal humans. Our nation is going through a major revolution of values and ideals, and we will *never* be the same again.

Change is scary and losing privilege and power often feels like a threat to your "equality" or "rights." It is no wonder that in the midst of these tumultuous times, a candidate like Donald Trump has risen to power with a simple message—restore the patriarchy to America. Keep the rich, white, straight, cisgender, Christian men comfortable and in power. Deport or imprison those who are threatening the patriarchal way of life. And of course, motivated by their fear, many have flocked to support Trump as a last-ditch effort to regain their privilege. This is the real meaning behind Trump's campaign slogan, "Make American *Great Again*." *Once* we were great and our nation needs to return to *those* values and morals (even though they were implicated in the oppression of women and minorities).

When we view the current events of our nation through this lens, everything becomes crystal clear. Nothing is as mysterious or perplexing as it once seemed. How could a candidate as unqualified, bombastic, and bigoted as Donald Trump ever rise to such a position of power and influence? It's simple. Threaten the privilege of society's "elite" and watch what happens. Watch the many creative ways privileged people try to regain their power—talk of "religious freedom," terrorism, and walls. And if that doesn't work, they ultimately will turn to anger and violence as a means of asserting their power and regaining control.

Donald Trump is the embodiment of American patriarchy, and his primary constituency are the fearful beneficiaries of that patriarchy, who are ready to do anything they can to keep true and lasting equality for *all* people from becoming a reality in our nation. For equality and justice for *all* means privilege for *none*, and that's not what this nation was *truly* founded on. In principle, America is a nation of progress and radical equality, to be sure. But in practice, we are culture of segregation, discrimination, and fear. But that day, I believe, is coming to an end. Before we taste true equality, though, we will first experience the backlash of those from whom privilege is slipping through their fingers. They will fight, they will cry "persecution," and they will ultimately lose. Little do they know that their loss is actually a win for *all* of us, including for *them*. For in that day, when white, straight, cisgender, wealthy, Christian men no longer secure power through the oppression of those who are different, we might truly discover the ability to be one nation, indivisible, with liberty and justice for all.

"Welcome to the Revolution"
January 31, 2017

For far too long, too many of us have allowed our complacency to keep us from acting. We fell into a trance, believing that things couldn't really get *that* bad. But then the unthinkable happened.

I often think back to election night in November. I had gathered together with a group of my LGBT+ friends at our local Democrat watch party expecting to spend the night celebrating a victory for progress. As the night went on and the numbers rolled in, one of my friends would frequently look at me and ask, "Brandan, is it time to start worrying yet?" I responded, "Of course not. There's no way that he's going to win." This exchanged happened a half-dozen times throughout the evening and after about an hour, we all decided that it would be best if we left the party and headed to a more private space to watch the election together. Sitting around a table, we silently watched the television screen as the numbers rolled in. Fear was palpable in the room. We couldn't eat, we couldn't drink, and we couldn't speak. After about another hour, we all decided it was time for us to go to bed.

The results seemed certain—an unqualified, immoral man who represented the antithesis of all of our hopes and values was about to take control of our nation. We never believed such a thing could really happen. Such a situation only seemed possible in the distant past, in the time of kings and dictators. Certainly, our civilized, evolved world couldn't return to such a time. And yet, when I woke up in the morning and looked down at my phone, the CNN news alert read, "Donald Trump will be the 45th President of the United States," and I fell back into the bed and wept.

My tears weren't because my political party lost. They weren't because I think that Republicans are indecent and dangerous. My tears came from the harsh realization that I had been living in a dream state, caught in a massive delusion that somehow our nation was better off than it truly was. I had imagined we had progressed much further than we did. I cried because I realized that there was a large group of folks across this country that still didn't believe I should have equal rights as an LGBT+ person. There was a large group of people that believe people of color should be marginalized or deported based on their religion or nationality. This was a group of people that I had completely isolated myself from and that I had forgot even existed.

I cried because my illusions of progress and change were stripped away over night, and the reality of just how much work was left to do overwhelmed me and kindled a deep fear that if we continued to fall back into the same trance-like state we would allow this illusion of progress to continue, while the deep roots of our nation's biggest hurdles continued to grow deeper still.

I cried because I was afraid that we would become complacent yet again.

A few months have passed since the election of Donald Trump, and I have to say that those tears and fears have all but evaporated. In the past few months, we have seen an unprecedented uprising of the American people from every race, religion, and socioeconomic status taking to the streets in every city, large and small, across our great land. We have seen the emergence of truly intersectional movements of justice, where the insular focus on only the issues that affect us have faded into a cry for justice for all people, not just our own. We have seen people of faith and of no faith at all unite to oppose the desecration of Native American sacred land, and hundreds of thousands of Americans flock to airports to demand that Muslim refugees be welcomed to our country with open arms.

My tears of fear have turned to tears of joy, because I believe that so many of us, once blinded by our bubbles and privilege, have been shaken out of our sleep and finally realized that if we don't stand up, speak out, and raise hell, then we truly could find ourselves living in dark and oppressive times. We have come together in opposition to the agenda of a man who represents the worst in our human nature—greed, prejudice, arrogance, exploitation, violence, and abuse—and are demanding that our government represent the best of our human nature—charity, generosity, grace, reconciliation, and love.

We have entered into a moment like we've never seen before. A moment of awakening and unification, a moment where the moral arc of the universe is truly being bent towards a more just and generous future.

We clearly have a long way to go, but I am convinced that the shift that has occurred across our nation and around our world is powerful enough to overcome the forces that seek to drive us back. We must all lean into this awakening and continue to question the complacency that will inevitably arise in our minds, knowing that if we sit down and shut up, the roots of injustice will only grow deeper. But if we stand up, speak up, and act up, we can truly transform the future and pave a path towards the more beautiful world our hearts know is possible.

In this age of great danger, may we also recover that profound and stubborn hope that has existed in the hearts of all of those great reformers and revolutionaries who have been able to envision a future beyond their present reality, and who fought tirelessly until we all approached that reality together. We are up against a lot of threats, to be sure, and when we overcome these obstacles, I can only imagine that we will find ourselves deeply united in heart, mind, and vision, standing on the brink of a new era of history where justice will truly roll forth like a river and love will truly win, after all. But until then, we must continue our fight for that brave new world.

Now, more than ever, I believe in our collective power to overturn evil and overcome injustice. Now, more than ever, I believe we can come together across our deepest divides and paint a picture of that common dream for a world that works for the good of us all. Now, more than ever, I believe that when we raise our voices on behalf of one another, we will create a force for good that cannot be stopped, even by the most powerful of opponents. Now, more than ever, I believe that our light will overcome the darkness that we have allowed to fester beneath the surface.

Now is the moment of awakening and progress.

Welcome to the revolution.

Appendix 2

"Why Your Rainbow Flag Isn't Enough"
August 16, 2018

A few years ago, I was invited to preach at a self-proclaimed LGBT+ inclusive church. It was one of the first times I had been invited into a pulpit since I had come out as an openly gay Christian, and I was deeply honored to find a place that would welcome me and my calling regardless of my sexuality. As I approached the church, I spotted a large rainbow flag hanging above the door—this sight was healing and exhilarating for me, a sign that I wouldn't have to be ashamed of who God made me to be as I entered into this space. As I approached the door, there was a sign outside that read "We celebrate diversity!"—another indicator that this church was leaning into the gospel's call to radical inclusion. When it came time for me to preach, I walked up to the pulpit and looked out at the congregation for the first time, and a stunning realization hit me like a wall of bricks: nearly *everyone* gathered in the space was a white, cisgender, gay man.

So much for diversity.

Since this experience years ago, I have noticed that so many progressive, inclusive churches find themselves in a similar place: they work hard to be inclusive of the LGBT+ community, which usually actually means the L&G community (lesbian and gay), and once they pass a resolution or appoint a gay leader, their commitment to inclusivity stops. While I would never want to minimize the importance of LGBT+ inclusive communities, the question inclusive faith communities must grapple with is whether or not we have *truly understood* the full implications of our claim to inclusion. If your community is dedicated to including only *one* marginalized group of people at the expense of others, can you truly claim to be inclusive?

Over the past five years, I have had the honor of working with churches and denominations around the world as they have journeyed towards LGBT+ inclusion, and as I have engaged in this hard work, it has become clear to me that the general understanding of inclusivity in Christian circles is severely deficient. We have failed to understand how systemic oppression actually works in our churches and society, and have failed to grasp the reality of intersectionality—that all oppression and marginalization is fundamentally tied together, and therefore, unless we are seeking the liberation and inclusion of *all* marginalized groups, we are actually failing to fully include *any* marginalized groups.

What I mean is this—the LGBT+ community is *incredibly* diverse. A large number of LGBT+ people who face marginalization for their sexuality or gender identity also face exclusion and discrimination because of their race, socioeconomic status, or disability (to name a few areas) and if we are not intentionally working on dismantling our communities' discriminatory and privileged postures towards these categories *at the same time* as we fight for inclusion of sexual and gender minorities, then we are not *truly inclusive* of the full LGBT+ community. In reality, we're actually only including a small, privileged portion of the LGBT+ community, and therefore are actually participating in the furthering of the oppression of *other* minority groups.

In my new book *True Inclusion*, I tackle the topic of how churches and communities can intentionally engage in the hard work of true inclusion, with practical stories and actionable steps that I have seen work in inclusive faith communities around the world. Towards the end of the book, I challenge faith leaders and community members to consider what the goal of the church is. Is it to become large numerically or is it to reflect the full diversity of God's creativity, and be a powerful beacon of healing and justice for the good of the world? The reality is that when a community commits to embracing a posture of radical inclusion, it is often making a decision to sacrifice numerical growth for the good of justice and liberation of the marginalized. But this is the call of Christ and is the cost of walking the path of liberation.

I conclude a chapter with the following words:

> I believe inclusive churches are in fact called to have revolving doors—continually welcoming new people in to discover what it means to be a part of a faith that promotes justice, and then sending them on their way

with our blessings. In this way, we prevent our community from becoming diluted by trying to offer everything to everyone, we encourage people to become the fully formed humans that God created them to be, and we continually have space and resources to help new people who are seeking a community of healing and restoration.

It's far easier for us to seek liberation and inclusion of *one* group of people—it's comfortable, easy to manage, and easy to market to a singular group. But the call of Christ and the commitment that inclusion demands is that we sacrifice egoic desire for larger communities and lean into the need for communities that are truly healing and transforming lives through the power of the gospel. If we are going to be faithful to the way of Jesus and lean into the full posture of inclusion, we must be engaged in intersectional inclusivity, always seeking to lift up and learn from diverse voices who will challenge and transform our communities into the powerful beacon of justice they're called to be. We must fight our desire to be comfortable, and lean in to the journey of liberation for ourselves and all people, which demands that we rethink our way of doing church and life together as a community.

The path to inclusion isn't easy. This is why many communities stop short of this high calling. A rainbow flag and a pride float *isn't* enough. We must always be working to transform our perspectives and ask "Who else isn't being embraced in our community?" and work to ensure that they have equal access to their rightful place at the table of God's grace. This is what true inclusion demands, and this is what it looks like to truly follow in the path of Jesus.

"Stand and Be Counted: On Religiously Motivated Bullying"
Huffington Post, October 19, 2017

I was backed into a corner in the gym, surrounded by a small group of boys and girls, shoving me and shouting, "*You look so gay!*" I didn't know what to say or what to do. I was terrified. As they continued to scream and laugh at me, making jokes about my hair, my voice, and my skinny jeans, I felt shame rush over my face. I didn't know why this was happening to me and didn't know how to make it stop. I jumped up, shoved my way through the crowd, and ran outside, where I collapsed behind a bush and wept.

This incident happened to me when I was fifteen and I was at my *youth group event* at a Baptist church in Baltimore, Maryland. This wasn't the first time something like this happened to me, nor would it be my last. From the earliest days of going to school, I remember being made fun of and physically assaulted for looking, acting, or sounding "gay," whatever that meant.

When I began attending a conservative Christian church at the age of twelve, things only got worse. Now the homophobic bullying I experienced was being justified, encouraged even, by church leaders who said they spoke on behalf of God. "Homosexuality is a sin," they preached, "but we should love the sinner and hate the sin." What that translated to, in reality, was exclude, harass, and marginalize the sinner until they either changed, until they left the church, or even worse.

Bullying is a real problem for LGBT+ youth in school. Studies shows that over 64 percent of LGBT+ identified youth fear going to school because of the vicious bullying that they have to face, and 31 percent of LGBT+ youth say that their school officials do nothing to keep them safe. Now imagine how severe the situation is for LGBT+ youth in conservative *religious* contexts, whether private schools or church youth groups.

While I haven't found an official study on these numbers, I would confidently suggest that an upward of 85–90 percent of LGBT+ youth in conservative religious environments live in fear of being bullied from their peers, families, and religious leaders alike, and most of those who face such torment will likely not be supported or defended by anyone in authority in the religious community.

Bullying happens because we have been conditioned by our environments to fear that which isn't perceived as "normative." It happens because the message has been ingested that says unless someone looks, acts, dresses, and loves in a certain culturally defined standard, they are abnormal and potentially dangerous. Bullying happens when we fail to treasure the gifts that diversity and individuality bestow upon our collective culture and cling to mythic conformist ideals. And it is safe to say that no community cultivates these mindsets and environments more than our religious communities.

I write this, by the way, as a religious leader. I am the Lead Pastor of a Christian church in San Diego, California. I have spent over a decade within religious communities and training to be a "religious professional," and over the course of my journey I have seen both the tremendous healing that communities of faith can bring and the tremendous harm that they can perpetuate.

Now, ask almost any conservative religious leader if they support the bullying of LGBT+ youth and *of course* they will say "Absolutely not." The problem is that when the fundamental ideology you perpetuate teaches that someone is *fundamentally flawed* because of an unchangeable part of their personhood, there is no way that your community can *not* perpetuate bullying. When children are taught that to be LGBT+ is to be deviant and that the LGBT+ rights movement is an affront to God (common teachings in conservative religious environments), how are they not supposed to translate that message into exclusion and bullying? What exactly does it look like to "love the sinner" while "hating their sin," when the so-called "sin" is a *part of their very identity*?

On this Spirit Day, I want to be unambiguous about this truth: If your church, family, school, or community teaches that to *be* LGBT+ is sinful, wrong, or unnatural, you are culpable for the torment that leads LGBT+ youth to be three times more likely to attempt suicide than other youth. Similarly, if your community refuses to take a stand in support of LGBT+ people, you are also culpable for the harm that is done to LGBT+ youth, for silence is complicity.

There is no room here for disagreement—to preach a message of exclusion is to preach a message that encourages bullying and marginalization. I've experienced it time and time again over the course of life within conservative religious environments, and I too have been driven to the brink of suicide because of the repetitive messages and behavior I experienced at the hands of religious leaders and people.

With all that we now know about human sexuality and gender identity, and with the prevalence of studies that show the impact of exclusive religious teaching and practice on LGBT+ people, it is no longer acceptable to promote these messages of harm and exclusion, and it's certainly not okay to remain unambiguous about where you stand. Jesus himself commanded, "Let your yes be yes and your no be no!" If you belong to a community that excludes, which in turn perpetuates harm to LGBT+ people, you must be willing to say it and own it, which is why I am so grateful for the work of a new organization called Church Clarity, which is putting pressure on churches across this country to clarify where they stand. Your people deserve to know, and LGBT+ youth deserve to be protected from the harm that will be done to them in non-affirming environments.

Likewise, those who stand as affirming religious allies of LGBT+ people must also stand and be counted, being unafraid to call out institutions and leaders that perpetuate harm and to be known as safe harbors and defenders of LGBT+ youth in their communities. These kids need us and our support. They need to know they are loved and will be stood up for in the face of homophobia, which is why I am grateful for organizations like Faith in America, which is bringing together thousands of people to defend LGBT+ youth and end homophobic teachings by religious institutions.

All in all, the suffering I experienced growing up within my religious context could have been and should have been avoided. The suffering of every LGBT+ person at the hands of those who exclude and demonize us should be avoided. But for that to happen, we need our allies to stand up, speak up, and act on our behalf. We need our churches and schools and families to be committed to our equality and our flourishing as vital parts of every community. We need to dispel any and all myths of "normality" with their calls for "conformity" and embrace the beautiful complexity that is humanity. We especially need religious institutions to acknowledge and own the harm they've perpetuated, publicly repent, and take tangible actions to ensure the inclusion and flourishing of the LGBT+ people in our midst.

This is the Spirit at the heart of all of our religious traditions anyway. The Spirit of love, of creativity, and of grace. And on this Spirit Day, it is my sincere hope, prayer, and call to every religious leader and every person of faith to take action on behalf of LGBT+ youth in your community. We owe it to them, and their very lives depend on it.

"The Harm of Conversion Therapy"
Huffington Post, February 28, 2017

The following is a transcript of my testimony to the Seventy-First General Assembly of the State of Colorado in support of House Bill 17-1156, which seeks to make conversion therapy on minors from licensed mental health professionals illegal in Colorado.
Good Afternoon mister chairman and committee.

My name is Brandan Robertson and I am an LGBT+ evangelical minister and author currently based here in Denver.

Four years ago, I was a senior studying at Moody Bible Institute in Chicago. During my senior year, I began to confess to a few trusted professors about my "struggle" with same-sex attraction. Very quickly, I was told that I needed to begin work to overcome this "sin" in my life. One professor ordered me a famous reparative therapy textbook and told me to begin reading it and reporting to her what I thought. She also very forcefully suggested I begin meeting with another professor for a very mild version of conversion therapy.

Every week for my entire senior year, I met with this professor who had studied the pseudo-psychology of conversion therapists. In addition to the program she offered me, she encouraged me to begin treatment with a number of *"licensed conversion therapists."* Every week I would come to my professors office and be asked to confess my "sinful" attractions, looking deep into my past to find the periods of abuse that made me gay, and using holy water, crucifixes, and intense prayer, we asked God to heal those wounds and to help me overcome these dangerous same-sex attractions.

Thankfully, being twenty years old at the time, I was able to find a supportive community in Chicago that helped me realize that what I was experiencing in these sessions was not only scientifically unfounded but psychologically harmful; I was able to maintain some degree of health and eventually, in 2015, come out as an openly LGBT+ evangelical.

For so many young people throughout Colorado, finding a community of support to counteract dangerous narratives and pseudo-science isn't an option. Studies are consistently showing that young people are coming out at earlier and earlier ages, and if they find themselves in a conservative Christian home, there is a high likelihood that they will be forced to participate in conversion therapy programs much more damaging and intense than what I experienced.

Studies show that LGBT+ youth that come from Christian homes are *significantly* more likely to attempt suicide than those who are not, because so many families have been fed false information by therapists about the development of sexual orientation and gender identity and the value of conversion therapy.

Because conversion therapy is framed as a matter of faith in God's ability to transform "sinful" struggles, so many parents cannot even entertain the idea that conversion therapy is harmful, because to do so would be a contradiction to their faith.

This leaves thousands of LGBT+ youth forced into these programs, either out of misinformation and deception, or against their will, and the damage that is done will take decades to work through and may even cost them their lives.

Today, I am here to support this bill, which will protect LGBT+ youth from dangerous and discredited practices that seek to change their God-given sexual orientation and gender identity. This bill is aimed at state-licensed therapists who are falsely claiming that being LGBT is a mental illness and who therefore take advantage of youth and their parents, doing immeasurable harm.

This is a human rights issue.

As an evangelical Christian, I am compelled to stand up for the voiceless and to speak truth to power. The LGBT+ youth across this nation, who have far too often been silenced by church leaders, parents, and therapists practicing this discredited version of therapy, need a voice. They deserve to be protected from being subjected to pseudo-therapy such as what I went through. They need lawmakers and faith leaders to stand up on their behalf and defend them from these destructive practices.

That's why I am here today. As one who has survived and is now thriving as both an evangelical and an openly LGBT+ person, I am here to let these youth know that there is hope for them. And I am here to ask you to not allow one more child or young person to be forcefully subjected to the damaging and discredited practices of conversion therapy. Lives are truly on the line, and we cannot continue to stand by while young people's futures are severely hindered by the damage done by licensed therapists practicing this irresponsible and disproven practice of conversion therapy.

Thank you so much for your time.

"Why Pride? An Explanation for Straight People" *Huffington Post,* June 2, 2017

June is national pride month, a month set aside to remember, celebrate, and empower queer people and our contributions to the flourishing of humanity. All across the country, LGBT+ people and our allies will be gathering for festivals, parades, parties, demonstrations, and marches that boldly proclaim that we are not ashamed of our queerness and that we will not be silent until we have achieved full freedom and equality in our society and *every* society around the world.

Yet during this month, there will also be a lot of pushback from the heterosexual communities and individuals who just don't understand what this whole pride thing is about. I cant tell you the number of times I have been cornered by straight people who look me in the eyes and say, *"I'm okay with you all being gay, but why do you have to flaunt it in the streets? You don't see straight people doing that!"*

To which I respond *"Bullshit."*

I mean that in the kindest, most sincere way possible. But straight and cisgender people are *the most visible people on planet earth*, not just because of their sheer numbers, but because their relationships, sexuality, and gender expressions are seen as the "normative" expressions and are therefore uplifted and repeated in every community around the country. Straight, cisgender people hold hands as they walk down the street without fear of getting accosted. They watch television shows and movies, listen to music, and read books that center on their relationships and gender expression. The majority of advertisements on billboards, websites, and television center on heterosexual and cisgender people. And our government is set up to privilege and favor heterosexual relationships above all others.

In short, straight people flaunt their straightness all day, every day, in every part of this country. And despite the far-right narrative that the "gays" are taking over our country, for a majority of LGBT+ people in America, it is still incredibly uncomfortable at best, dangerous at worst, for us to express ourselves in our communities. In a majority of states across our country, our rights and dignity are not fully protected by the law, and, in fact, there are fierce movements that seek to oppress and marginalize us and our relationships.

So, while we have seen tremendous progress in the fight for LGBT+ equality, inclusion, and rights in the United States, the reality is that we are incredibly far from being fully equal in every realm of society. And that is why pride is so important.

For many LGBT+ people, pride is the *one time* of the year that they can be out and proud of who they are and who they love. It's the one time of year that we can stand boldly in the streets with droves of other queer individuals, proclaiming that we are fully human and deserve to be celebrated and uplifted just like everyone else. Even in cities that are seen as LGBT+ friendly, it is still an incredibly healing experience to get to march in parades or attend festivals where thousands upon thousands of LGBT+ people are letting their lights shine before all people without fear. Pride is often the beginning of the process of healing from the trauma inflicted on us by our heterosexist, patriarchal society. Pride is a time where we step out of the shadows and declare that we will no longer forced to suppress our truest selves because of heterosexual fragility and fear.

Now, of course, in the midst of all of the deeper causes and meanings behind pride, it is also, most importantly, a time of celebration. It's a time to party, to relax, and to let loose in public, which is something that heterosexual and cisgender people get to do every single day of the year, but something that LGBT+ people simply *don't* get to do. So yes, people of all shapes, sizes, religions, ethnicities, races, and cultures will be marching through the streets shirtless, and perhaps even pantless (hello speedos!), but this has a lot less to do with LGBT+ being hyper-sexual or promiscuous; instead, it's a radical display of liberation and safety, a time to let our bodies and lives be seen as the beautiful displays of creativity and majesty that they are—something, again, that straight people get to see and do every single day.

Pride marches and festivals were started as subversive displays of light in the midst of the darkness of heternormitivty and hatred, and today, for many if not most LGBT+ people, they still retain this important meaning and power. Though they may look like giant parties in the street, take a second and think about what it feels like to march through a city, freely expressing who you are, whom you love, and what you desire for the first time without fearing that you'll be accosted, abused, or mocked. Think about all of the children and teenagers who know they are LGBT+ but cannot even begin to fathom taking a step out of the closet for fear of abuse from their families, churches, or peers, who look out at those celebrating pride and see a glimpse of hope that things can get better, and that they can be free, safe, and celebrated for who they are. That is the power of pride, and that's why pride month is so damn important.

So, if you're a straight person and you're finding yourself perplexed by the pride celebrations taking place in your city this year, stop and remember that you get to live out and proud every single day without fear, without oppression, and without even thinking about it. That is a unique gift that majority of LGBT+ people have never gotten to experience. Think about all of the hurdles to equality that still exist in our nation, and the trauma that so many LGBT+ people have faced simply because of who they are or who they love. And as you reflect on the reality of LGBT+ people, I hope you begin to realize the importance and power of pride, and perhaps will even decide to pick up a rainbow flag and stand on the sidelines cheering on your local LGBT+ community as they fearlessly express their beauty in your community.

> "When all Americans are treated as equal, no matter who they are or whom they love, we are all more free."
>
> —President Barack Obama

"There Is No Fear in Love: My Experience Trying to Pray the Gay Away"
Patheos, November 30, 2018

As I entered into the professor's office, I was trembling. Dr. Rose was known to be one of the fiercest, most opinionated professors on campus who happily called out students by name in her classes for disagreeing with her political or theological views. I was being called in because she was "gravely concerned" about my presence at Moody Bible Institute where I was finishing up my Junior year of studies. I walked in and sat down in a chair in the corner of the dimly lit office, and Dr. Rose turned and looked at me with fierceness in her eyes. "You've gotten away with murder. I think they're going to let you graduate, but I have been fighting it with all of my might. You are a deceiver, a liar, you are being used by Satan to lead a whole caravan of folks straight to hell. You should be ashamed.

If you had any integrity at all, you'd drop out now and pay back your scholarships and move on." "But, Dr. Rose, I don't think you understand, I'm just trying to be honest. I'm still a Christian!" I responded, tears welling up in my eyes. "I just believe it's okay to talk to people who believe different things than we do."

Dr. Rose had called me to her office on this day because she had been told by another professor that I was struggling with same-sex attraction and on top of that had begun interviewing a number of popular, well-known, gay-affirming pastors on my podcast and campus radio show. They believed I was going to start advocating for LGBT+ inclusion on campus and promoting theology that contradicted Moody's official position, when in reality, I was still quite conservative and still firmly believed that my same-sex attraction was sinful. But simply because I was talking to people with different perspectives, I was deemed to be not just dangerous, but demonic.

"If you want to prove yourself to us, you need to start meeting with Dr. Gene, her office is right next door to mine. She practices healing prayer, which God can use to heal you of your sexuality." I quickly replied, "Of course, I'll do anything," and I really meant it. I was not trying to cause trouble, and I certainly didn't want to lead myself or anyone else astray. "And here is a book I want you to read and report back to me on. It's by the leading therapist that deals with your issue." Dr. Rose handed me a brick of a book called *Shame and Attachment Loss* by Dr. Joseph Nicolosi, one of the most influential reparative therapists in the country. "I'll do it," I said. "I'm really sorry, Dr. Rose." She turned away from me and I fumbled towards the door of her office, visibly shaking, with tears running down my face.

The next day, I had my first meeting with Dr. Gene, the professor who specialized in healing prayer. I had only seen her around campus a few times, but she struck me as a stereotypical lesbian—tall, athletically built, with short hair and a deep voice. I walked into her office, which was adorned with crucifixes and paintings of Christ on the cross. She closed the door gently and said, "It's good to meet you, Brandan. I've heard you've been raising a bit of hell around here." She smiled and laughed. "I really haven't been trying to," I said with a slight grin. "Moody can be a little intense sometimes. So, tell me, why are you here?" For the next half an hour, I shared about my upbringing with an abusive, alcoholic father and an over-attached mother, I spoke of my same-sex attractions and my struggles with masturbation. I poured everything out for Dr. Gene, deeply hoping that she could offer some assistance to me.

As soon as I finished, Dr. Gene looked at me again with a gentle smile and said, "Do you mind if I lay hands on you and pray?" I nodded. She then led me in one of the most profound prayers I have ever experienced. "Brandan, as we sit in the presence of God, identify a time when you were an infant where you were neglected." I imagined a scene my mom had told me about, where I was left crying in a crib for hours while my dad was passed out drunk. As I conjured up images of that scene in my mind, Dr. Gene prompted me to imagine Jesus stepping in to my room, lifting me up out of the crib, and embracing me in his arms. "Can you feel his heart beating against your body?" she asked. "I can. I feel so much peace" I replied. She then prayed for God to pour healing into my young soul, to break the chains of pain and generational curses that were upon me and begin restoring me to be the whole man I was meant to be.

Towards the end of the prayer, Dr. Gene reached for a bottle of water sitting on her bookshelf. She said, "Do you mind if I use some holy water?" I was taken aback. We were a conservative Baptist college that was decidedly anti-Catholic. We didn't use holy water. But, being the edgy boundary-pusher that I was, I thought it would be a cool experience. "Sure," I replied. She poured water on my head and declared that I was clean before God and that my chains were being broken. She invited me to renounce all of the demonic spirits that were trying to overcome me, "Repeat after me: I renounce Baal, Ashtoreth, the spirit of homosexuality, the curse of my father . . . ." Moment after moment, I renounced everything she told me to, and as the prayers got more impassioned, I felt tingles all over my body. By the time she said "Amen," I opened my eyes and had tears of joy. I felt like a new man. "Thank you so much, Dr.

Appendix 2

Gene" I exclaimed. "Anytime. Shall we meet at this same time next week?" "I will be here!"

I left her office feeling on cloud nine, like God was actually going to heal me, not just from my same-sex attraction but from all of the pain in my life. I felt like I had been saved all over again and was so eager to get back into her office next week for more prayer. Every week, we would have a similar experience where I would share a little bit more about my "sin struggles" and Dr. Gene would open up to me a bit about hers, and we'd pray intensely for healing. A deep relationship began to develop, as you'd expect to happen with someone who you are sharing your most intimate thoughts and struggles with. Dr. Gene and I began to text outside of class, whenever I felt tempted by homosexuality or pornography, I would text her and she'd send me a powerfully worded prayer. She became an advocate for me with Dr. Rose and the Dean of Students, who were keeping their eye on me as I continued to blog and podcast.

About four months into my healing prayer treatment, I had what I called a "major stumble." I had invited my best friend Max home with me for the holidays—we both struggled with same-sex attraction. One morning as we were waking up, we began to kiss and fondle each other. This lasted for all of five minutes, but as soon as we stopped, we both filled with dread. "What have we done?" I whispered loudly, so my parents couldn't hear. "Let's pray" Max said. We fell to our knees by the bedside and repented, begging God to forgive us and to keep us from this sinful behavior. As soon as we finished, I texted Dr. Gene to let her know what had happened and to ask her to pray. She called my phone and I explained the situation. She rebuked me firmly, told me to keep my distance from my friend for the rest of my trip, and prayed over me. When I got off the phone, I told Max what she had said, and he agreed. We barley talked the rest of the trip, and anytime I got in physical proximity to him, he would turn and say, "Get away from me."

I reflected on this experience for the next couple of days before we drove back to Chicago. What happened between us didn't feel wrong, but I knew it was wrong because God's word said so.

The relational separation between us, the rebuke I received, it all felt like a harsh overreaction. This whole thing felt "off." But I couldn't express that, and I fought against these thoughts in my head. "This is just the devil tempting me," I deduced. But when we got back to Chicago, Dr. Gene told Max and I that we needed to deal with our sin more severely, so she booked us a session with one of the leading "healing prayer" practitioners at Church of the Resurrection in Wheaton, IL, the home base of this healing prayer movement.

It was a cold, gray Chicago morning when Max and I made our way to the train station to go out to Wheaton. We didn't say much to each other and intended to keep our distance so as not to tempt each other to sin. I felt sick to my stomach the entire hour-long train ride to the suburbs, wondering what we were about to experience when we arrived at the church. When we walked into the large, empty church building, we were greeted by four individuals, including one of the most prominent authors and leaders of the healing prayer movement. They welcomed us and took us to a small office where they sat us next to each other and told us to describe, in detail, what we had done with each other, and our current sin-struggles.

Max and I sat awkwardly in silence. "You want me to say this out loud?" Max said to the counselors. "Yes, unless we can name our sin, bring it into the light, there will be no healing," one replied. So Max began to describe what happened at my house over holiday break in vivid detail. He then spoke of the sexual tension that had been building between us since freshmen year, and his other struggles. I reluctantly followed suit, naming each of my struggles, my own emotions about Max, and my desire to be healed. They looked at us with concern. "You're going to have to make some big changes, gentlemen. First, your friendship is over." A knot formed in my stomach and a lump arose in my throat. I began to weep. Max was my best friend—he knew everything about me, and I admired him so much. I wasn't sure how I could continue to make it through Bible college without him.

"Next, we're going to spend some time praying for both of you individually. Brandan come with me." I followed a slender man with a salt-and-pepper beard into an adjacent office. He asked me to stand up tall, as he pressed his hand onto my back. He looked at me in the eyes and said, "Do you want to be healed?" I wiped away my tears, breathed deeply, and said "Yes, I really do."

His assistant grabbed a bottle of holy water and he began to anoint my head, praying that God would cleanse my mind. He anointed my chest, asking for God to cleanse my heart. He poured water on my pelvic region and prayed for God to heal my sexual desires. And out of nowhere he put his hands on my head and began to shout in tongues, an unintelligible "language" given to individuals by God. He vacillated between shouting in gibberish, and then renounced Satan and various demonic forces in English. I stood with my eyes closed shaking in fear. I didn't feel God's presence here at all. I didn't feel like I was being healed. In fact, this felt demonic to me. This man didn't know what he was doing. He had made me feel ashamed and uncomfortable. As I stood listening to him shout gibberish over me, I felt anger rising within me. This was *absolute bullshit.*

When they finally finished praying, they dismissed Max and me and told us that we should plan on visiting them again soon. We walked quietly through the small town of Wheaton, back to the train, and headed back into the city. Max and I wouldn't talk again for a few months. I entered into such a deep season of darkness—losing my best friend, whom I loved so deeply, and beginning to realize that this healing prayer thing wasn't working and facing the fact that if I didn't keep doing this, I would likely not be able to graduate. The pressure landed me in the hospital just a few weeks later after suffering a massive panic attack in the middle of the night. I awoke unable to breathe, overwhelmed with grief and shame, feeling like something must be deeply wrong with me for this not to work. All I wanted was to be faithful to God. All I wanted was to do what was right. But nothing seemed to work. Nothing seemed to help.

I continued to meet with Dr. Gene every week, trying to be authentic in our sessions, but growing increasingly cynical with Moody and this whole process. She could see that something was off, but continued to pray, anoint me with holy water, and hope that God would do something to heal me. By the time May rolled around, Dr. Gene had assured me that when she was asked about whether I should be permitted to graduate that she had given her endorsement, but that she remained concerned that I hadn't experienced more healing or progress.

During our graduation ceremony, Dr. Gene prayed the final prayer over the graduating class, and I felt like she was looking at me the entire time: "God, keep them from the snares of sin, and lead them into wholeness and holiness"—this had, indeed, been my hope and my desire. But nothing about my experience seemed to have been holy or leading me towards wholeness—the rejection and demonization by professors and students alike, the consistent shaming of me for my attractions, the destruction of my deepest relationships had pushed me further from God and had made me more cynical towards evangelicalism than ever before. My faith was in a shambles, and I feared that my life would soon be as well.

Six months later, I had moved home to Washington, DC and had taken a job for a new organization called "Evangelicals for Marriage Equality," a group advocating for civil marriage equality among evangelicals. In my time out of school, I had discovered that there were large groups of Christians that were much more gracious, kind, and affirming of who I was, even as I continued to wrestle to reconcile my faith and sexuality and had become passionate about seeking to bridge the divide between the LGBT+ community and evangelicals. As stories about my work began to surface in the national media, I began to hear from students and professors at Moody.

"Dr. Rose spent half of the class warning us about you today, Brandan," one student texted me. "For what? Arguing for civil rights?" I responded. I was familiar with the way Moody demonized students who left their campus and then didn't continue to align with their social and theological views. I just hoped that students would be wise enough not to buy into whatever demonization narrative was being spun about me. A few days later, I opened up my inbox and saw a name that made the color drain from my face. It was Dr. Gene. The following is an excerpt of that email:

> Hi Brandan,
>
> The last time we talked you . . . acknowledged that you were slothful, and simply declined to exercise your will to stop sinning. You were dishonest about your commitments, among other things, hiding your commitment to heretical views. On atonement, for example. I wonder whether in your very expensive talks you tell the people how dishonest, cunning, and manipulative you are. I wonder whether you tell them about your addictions and compulsions. I wonder whether you tell them about how actively you cultivate a sin life while being so inactive towards righteousness and how damningly lazy you are? Do you tell them how disinterested you are in the Word? Or how driven to power you are, desiring spiritual gifts for public display? So where exactly do the bridges you allegedly build lead? Certainly, you are a leader, Brandan. It is safe to say that in the current trajectory of your life you will usher many into a hellish existence. And when you need the blood of Christ to wash away your sins, where will you turn, now that you have renounced His redeeming and transforming work so thoroughly? I know you like to be coddled. True words feel so harsh to you. (This, of course, keeps the door to your personal prison locked.) Nevertheless, only one word makes sense to speak: Repent."

As I read this email for the first time, I surprised myself when I didn't experience anger. I wasn't intimidated. No, as I read these words, I felt *truly sorry* for Dr. Gene. I felt sorry for so many of my professors at Moody. I felt sorry for those who had committed their lives to trying to pray the gay out of people. Every line of this email was infused with fear. This was the same fear that drove students and faculty to fear me talking to people with different perspectives. It was the same fear that caused me and Max to sever our relationship. It was the same fear that had landed me in the hospital. It was the same fear that made me want to give up on faith altogether. And I remembered the words of Scripture in 1 John 4:16–18, which says:

> God is love. Whoever lives in love lives in God, and God in them. This is how love is made complete among us so that we will have confidence on the day of judgment: In this world, we are like Jesus. There is no fear in love. But perfect love drives out fear, because fear has to do with punishment. The one who fears is not made perfect in love.

Every attempt to change my sexuality was rooted in fear. Every harsh word and threat of expulsion emerged from a posture of fear. Everything about my faith as an evangelical Christian found its genesis in fear of hell, fear of judgment, and ultimately fear of God. But now, standing on the other side of these traumatic experiences and attempts to heal myself, I felt, for the first time, a deep sense of love. Not sentimental love, but an enduring sense that I was embraced by God and that regardless of what I believed or did, nothing could separate me from this love. I realized, for the first time, that the evangelical faith that feared difference and sought to change it was rooted in fear and therefore, could not be said to come from God, for "the one who fears is not made in perfect love."

As I recount my experience trying to find healing from who God made me to be, and as I hear the stories of individuals who went through far worse than I did, my heart continues to break. It breaks because of how deceived these Christians are who do not know the enduring love available to them to free them from living in fear. It breaks because of how many LGBT+ Christians end up destroying or ending their lives because of the pressure that fear-mongering Christians pile upon them. It breaks because so many of these Christians will never get to experience the liberation that I have tasted by discovering the truth of the words written in 1 John—love does indeed expel all fear.

The love I share with my partners of the same-sex is liberating. The love I get to proclaim every week as an openly gay

Christian pastor heals the deepest of wounds. The love that I feel for myself, as a gay man created in the image and likeness of God, has set me free from the chains of bondage and shame. The life I now live is filled with so much joy and peace—I feel like I've been born again. I only hope that those still living in the bondage of fear will taste of this love and be liberated to be the people God made them to be, too.

Bibliography

Anderson, Cheryl. *Ancient Laws and Contemporary Controversies: The Need for Inclusive Biblical Interpretation.* Oxford: Oxford University Press, 2009.

Apulieus. *Golden Ass.* Translated by Robert Graves. New York: Farrar, Straus & Giroux, 1951.

Ateek, Naim Stifan. *A Palestinian Theology of Liberation.* New York: Orbis, 2017.

Auburn Seminary. *Being in Relationship.* 6 December 2018. Online: auburnseminary.org/wp-content/uploads/2018/11/BIR-online-final.pdf.

Berlin, Adele, and David Stern, eds. *The Jewish Study Bible.* Oxford: Oxford University Press, 2004.

Boscoe-Huffman, Scott, et al. "Religious Belief and Perceptions of Psychological Health in LGBT Individuals." Online: https://www.researchgate.net/profile/Louis_Hoffman/publication/260002146_Religious_Belief_and_Perceptions_of_Psychological_Health_in_LGBT_Individuals/links/0a85e52f00dd10ca98000000.pdf

Brownfeld, Allen. "It Is Time to Confront the Exclusionary Ethnocentrism in Jewish Sacred Literature." *Issues* Winter 2000, 10.

Carter, J. Cameron. *Race: A Theological Account.* Oxford: Oxford University Press, 2008.

Cheng, Patrick. *Radical Love: An Introduction to Queer Theology.* New York: Seabury, 2011.

Cicero, Marcus Tullius. *Pro Rabirio Postumo.* Translated by Mary Siani-Davies. Oxford: Clarendon, 2001.

Cone, James. *God of the Oppressed.* New York: Orbis, 2000.

Craig, John. "Wesleyan Baccalaureate Is Delivered by Dr. King." *Hartford Courant,* June 8, 1964, 4.

Day, John. "Does the Old Testament Refer to Sacred Prostitution and Did It Actually Exist in Ancient Israel?" In *Biblical and Near Eastern Essays: Studies in Honour of Kevin J. Cathcart,* edited by Carmel McCarthy and John Healey, 2–21. New York: Continuum, 2004.

Department of Women's Studies. "The History of Patriarchy." *University of Colorado,* 13 February 2015. Online: www.colorado.edu/wrc/2015/02/13/history-patriarchy.

DeYmaz, Mark. *Disruption: Repurposing the Church to Redeem the Community.* Nashville, TN: Thomas Nelson, 2017.

Dover, Kenneth. *Greek Homosexuality.* Cambridge: Harvard University Press, 1978.

Figueroa, V., and F. Tasker. "'I always have the idea of sin in my mind . . .': Family of Origin, Religion, and Chilean Young Gay Men." *Journal of GLBT Family Studies* 10.3 (2013) 269–97.

Flood, Derek. *Disarming Scripture: Cherry-Picking Liberals, Violence-Loving Conservatives, and Why We All Need to Learn to Read the Bible Like Jesus Did.* San Francisco: Metanoia, 2014.

Frilingos, "Sexing the Lamb." In *New Testament Masculinities*, edited by Stephen Moore and Janice Anderson, 297–318. Semeia Studies 45. Atlanta: Society of Biblical Literature; 2003.

Gagnon, Robert A. J. *The Bible and Homosexual Practice: Text and Hermeneutics.* Nashville, TN: Abingdon, 2001.

Goldbach, Jeremy. "Growing Up Queer and Religious: A Quantitative Study Analyzing the Relationship between Religious Identity Conflict and Suicide in Sexual Minority Youth." Paper presented at the 141st APHA Annual Meeting and Exposition. University of Southern California, 2013.

Gonnerman, Joshua. "Why Matthew Vines Is Wrong about thw Bible and Homosexuality." *First Things*, 11 October 2012. Online: https://www.firstthings.com/web-exclusives/2012/10/why-matthew-vines-is-wrong-about-the-bible-and-homosexuality.

Goodacre, Mark. *The Synoptic Problem: A Way through the Maze.* London: T. & T. Clark, 2001.

Handley, Paul. "Primates Distance Themselves from the US Episcopal Church in Official Statement." *The Church Times*, 14 January 2016. Online: www.churchtimes.co.uk/articles/2016/22-january/news/uk/primates-distance-themselves-from-the-us-episcopal-church-in-official-statement.

Hartke, Austen. *Transforming: The Bible in the Lives of Transgender Christians.* Louisville, KY: Westminster John Know, 2018.

Hays, Richard B. "Awaiting the Redemption of Our Bodies." In *Homosexuality and the Church*, edited by Jeffrey Silker, 3–17. Louisville, KY. WJK, 1994.

Hess, Carol Lakey. *Caretakers of Our Common House: Women's Development in Communities of Faith.* Nashville: Abingdon, 1997.

"The History of Patriarchy." *University of Colorado*, Department of Women's Studies, 13 February 2015. Online: www.colorado.edu/wrc/2015/02/13/history-patriarchy.

Holtz, Barry. *Back to the Sources: Reading the Classic Jewish Texts.* New York: Simon & Schuster, 2006.

Human Rights Campaign. "Policy and Position Statements on Conversion Therapy." *Human Rights Campaign* 2012. Online: http://www.hrc.org/resources/policy-and-position-statements-on-conversion-therapy.

Bibliography

Jerome. Letter XXII. In *Letters and Select Works*, translated W. H. Fremantle. *Select Library of Nicene and Post-Nicene Fathers*, Series 2, Vol. VI. Edinburgh: T. & T. Clark, 1892.

Jewish Press Staff. "Study: Highest Suicide Rates among Religious Homosexuals." *Jewish Press* 2012. Online: http://www.jewishpress.com/news/breaking-news/study-highest-rate-of-suicide-among-religious-homosexuals/2012/09/05/.

Kalir, Doron M. "Same-Sex Marriage and Jewish Law: Time for a New Paradigm?" Working paper. Cleveland State University, 2015. Online: https://engagedscholarship.csuohio.edu/cgi/viewcontent.cgi?referer=https://www.google.com/&httpsredir=1&article=1815&context=fac_articles.

Keen, Karen. *Scripture, Ethics, and the Possibility of Same-Sex Relationships*. Grand Rapids: Eerdmans, 2018.

Kirk, J. R. Daniel. "Eschatological Trajectory of Gay Inclusion." *Patheos*, 10 March 2016. Online: www.patheos.com/blogs/storiedtheology/2016/03/10/eschatological-trajectory-of-gay-inclusion/.

———. "Trajectories toward Gay Inclusion?" *Patheos*, 27 February 2016. Online: www.patheos.com/blogs/storiedtheology/2016/02/27/trajectories-toward-gay-inclusion/.

Kramer, Samuel Noah. *The Sacred Marriage Rite: Aspects of Faith, Myth and Ritual in Ancient Sumer*. Indianapolis, IN: Indiana University Press, 1969.

Kuruvilla, Carol. "Chilling Study Sums Up Link between Religion and Suicide for Queer Youth." *The Huffington Post*, 19 April 2018. Online: www.huffingtonpost.com/entry/queer-youth-religion-suicide-study_us_5ad4f7b3e4b077c89ceb9774.

Lillback, Peter, Vern Poythress, Iain M. Duguid, G. K. Beale, and Richard B. Gaffin. *Seeing Christ in All of Scripture: Hermeneutics at Westminster Theological Seminary*. Philadelphia: Westminster Seminary Press, 2016.

Loader, William. "Biblical Perspectives on Homosexuality and Leadership." *Murdoch University*, February 2008. Online: http://wwwstaff.murdoch.edu.au/~loader/LoaderBibPerspectives.pdf.

———. "What Does the Bible Say about Homosexuality?" Murdoch University. Online: wwwstaff.murdoch.edu.au/~loader/homosexuality.html.

Marcovich, Miroslav. "From Ishtar to Aphrodite." *Journal of Aesthetic Education* 30.2 (1996) 43–59.

Martin, Colby. "The Newest Non-LGBTQ-Affirming Approach: Reviewing Preston Sprinkle's 'Center for Faith, Sexuality, & Gender.'" October 3, 2018. Online: https://www.colbymartinonline.com/blog/2018/10/2/the-newest-non-lgbtq-affirming-approach-reviewing-preston-sprinkles-center-for-faith-sexuality-amp-gender.

McGrath, Alister. *Christian Theology: an Introduction*. Oxford: Wiley Blackwell, 2017.

Moltmann, Jürgen. "Jesus and the Kingdom of God." *The Asbury Theological Journal* 48.1 (1993) 5–18.

Bibliography

Moxnes, Halvor. *Putting Jesus in His Place: A Radical Vision of Household and Kingdom.* Louisville, KY: Westminster John Knox, 2003.

Nicholas, Ray. "Lesbian, Gay, Bisexual, and Transgender Youth: An Epidemic of Homelessness." *National Gay and Lesbian Task Force Policy Institute,* 2007. Online: http://www.thetaskforce.org/reports_and_research/homeless_youth.

Noll, Mark. *The Civil War as a Theological Crisis.* Chapel Hill, NC: University of North Carolina Press, 2015.

Philo. *On Flight and Findings.* Translated by Peter Kirby. Online: www.earlychristianwritings.com/yonge/book19.html.

Punt, Jeremy. "Romans 1:18–32 amidst the Gay-Debate: Interpretive Options." *HTS Teologiese Studies/Theological Studies* 63.3 (2007) 965–82.

Robertson, Brandan. *Our Witness: The Unheard Stories of LGBT+ Christians.* Eugene, OR: Cascade Books, 2017.

———. *True Inclusion: Creating Communities of Radical Embrace.* St. Louis, MO: Chalice, 2018.

Rohr, Richard. *The Universal Christ.* New York: Convergence, 2019.

Roller, Lynn. *In Search of God the Mother: The Cult of Anatolian Cybele.* Berkeley: University of California Press, 1999.

Silberman, Lou Hackett, and Haim Zalman Dimitrovsky. "Talmud and Midrash." *Encyclopædia Britannica,* 5 July 2016. Online: www.britannica.com/topic/Talmud.

Swancutt, Diana. *Toward a Theology of Eros.* New York: Fordham University Press, 2006.

———. "Still before Sexuality: 'Greek' Androgyny, the Roman Imperial Politics of Masculinity and the Roman Invention of the Tribas." In *Mapping Gender in Ancient Religious Discourses,* edited by Todd Penner and Caroline Vander Stichele, 11–61. Leiden: Brill, 2007.

Tashman, Brian. "Michael Brown: Gays Use Youth Suicide Victims as 'Pawns.'" *Right Wing Watch* 27 January 2012. Online: http://www.rightwingwatch.org/post/michael-brown-gays-use-youth-suicide-victims-as-pawns/.

Tombs, David. "Crucifixion, State Terror, and Sexual Abuse: Text and Context." Otago, NZ: University of Otago, 2018. Online: https://ourarchive.otago.ac.nz/bitstream/handle/10523/8558/Tombs%202018%20-%20Crucifixion%2C%20State%20Terror%2C%20and%20Sexual%20Abuse%20-%20Text%20and%20Context.pdf?sequence=1&isAllowed=y.

———. "#HimToo—Why Jesus Should Be Recognised as a Victim of Sexual Violence." 23 March 2018. Online: http://theconversation.com/himtoo-why-jesus-should-be-recognised-as-a-victim-of-sexual-violence-93677.

Townsley, Jeramy. "Paul, the Goddess Religions, and Queer Sects: Romans 1:23–28." *Journal of Biblical Literature* 130.4 (2011) 707–28.

Walsh, Jerome, T. "Leviticus 18:22 and 20:13: Who is Doing What to Whom?" *Journal of Biblical Literature* 120.2 (2001) 201–9.

Walters, Jonathan. "Invading the Roman Body: Manliness and Impenetrability in Roman Thought." In *Roman Sexualities*, edited by Judith P. Hallett and Marilyn B. Skinner, 29–46. Princeton: Princeton University Press, 1997.

Webb, William. "The Limits of a Redemptive-Movement Hermeneutic: A Focused Response to T. R. Schreiner." *Evangelical Quarterly* 75.4 (2003) 327–42.

———. *Slaves, Women & Homosexuals: Exploring the Hermeneutics of Cultural Analysis*. Downers Grove, IL: Intervarsity, 2001.

Yuan, Christopher. *Giving a Voice to the Voiceless: A Qualitative Study of Reducing Marginalization of Lesbian, Gay, Bisexual and Same-Sex Attracted Students at Christian Colleges and Universities*. Eugene, OR: Wipf & Stock, 2016.

Made in the USA
Coppell, TX
25 April 2021